Mythology for Students: Greek, Egyptian, Norse

Craig Whitmore

Bakersfield, CA

ISBN 978-1-257-83729-8

First Edition

What is mythology?

Mythology is a branch of knowledge dealing with the collection, study and understanding of myths or fables. It sometimes involves supernatural events or characters to explain the nature of the universe and humanity. The word mythology comes from the Greek language and means `"story-telling". Myths often explain universal and/or local beginnings, natural phenomena, inexplicable cultural rituals, and anything else for which no simple explanation presents itself.

Why study Greek, Egyptian, and Norse mythologies?

Three quick remarks about how this book looks at mythology are in order. Most importantly, students should realize that the term mythology does not, by itself, mean something is either true or false. Next, these versions of the mythology stories have been modified for the average 7th or 8th grade student. Students that wish to go further in their studies of mythology should realize that many original stories were written for an older audience. Finally, the mythologies covered in this book (Egyptian, Greek, and Norse) were chosen for three important reasons. First, none of these mythologies are still extant, that is, they are not believed in by any people group (unlike Hinduism, for instance). Second, all three of these have agreed upon pantheons (groups of gods and goddesses) and established stories with only small variations (unlike American Indian beliefs). Third, the English language has borrowed many recognizable terms from these three mythologies and these terms tend to come up quite often on state and national exams.

Web Sites for More Information *(if the hyperlink is broken, try Googling the website's title)*

http://www.pantheon.org/ *Encyclopedia Mythica* (lots of info)

http://www.abc.net.au/arts/wingedsandals/ *Winged Sandals* (nice Greek site with games)
http://www.mythweb.com/ *Myth Web* (very visual Greek info)
http://www.logicmazes.com/theseus.html Thesus & Minotaur maze game

www.ancientegypt.co.uk/life/activity/act_main.html *Play Senet Online* (cool flash game)

http://www.pbs.org/wgbh/nova/vikings/runes.html Viking Names in Runes
http://www.bbc.co.uk/history/ancient/vikings/launch_gms_viking_quest.shtml *Viking Quest* (very cool game)
http://www.mnh.si.edu/vikings/start.html Viking Informational site
http://www.bbc.co.uk/schools/vikings/index.shtml viking info site

GREEK STORIES

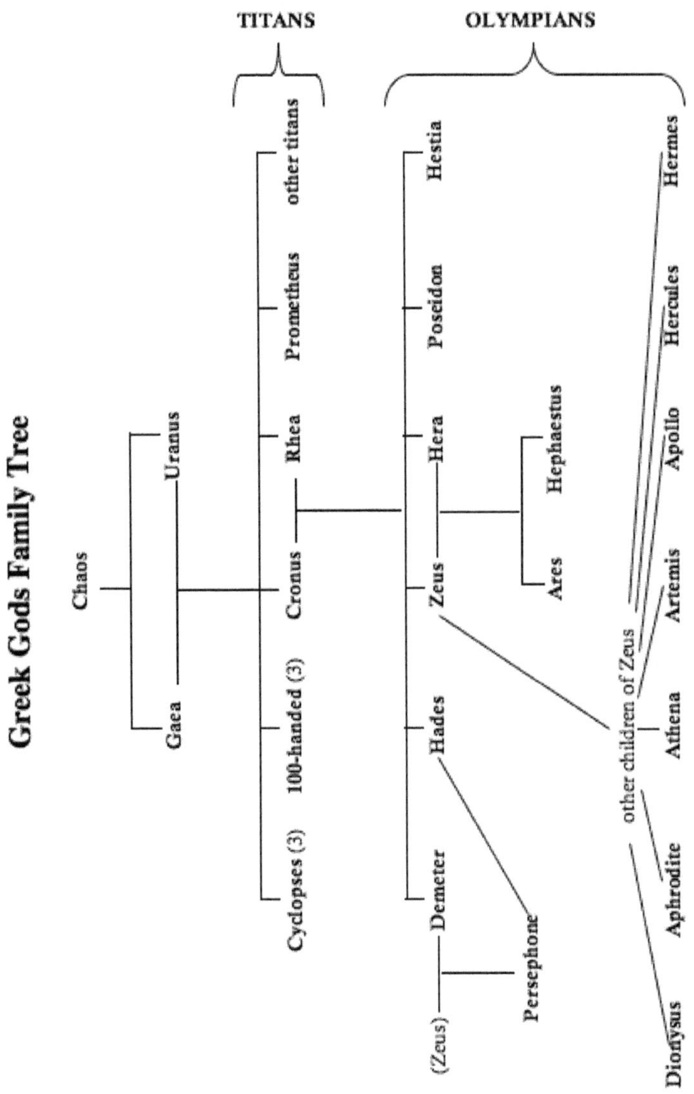
Greek Gods Family Tree
Chaos
Gaea
Uranus
TITANS
Cyclopses (3)
100-handed (3)
Cronus
Rhea
Prometheus
other titans
OLYMPIANS
Demeter
Hades
Zeus
Hera
Poseidon
Hestia
(Zeus)
Persephone
Ares
Hephaestus
other children of Zeus
Dionysus
Aphrodite
Athena
Artemis
Apollo
Hercules
Hermes

Greek Mythology Stories

Creation

At the dawn of creation, so the Greek poets say, there was only Chaos. The first thing in existence, Chaos was a swirling tempest, full of both darkness and light, enclosing everything there would ever be. In time Gaia, the earth, emerged from Chaos. Gaia was the earth-mother and she was the earth itself. All life sprang from her. Gaia gave birth to the heavens, Uranus, the first and greatest of the old gods.

In time, Gaia and Uranus became husband and wife. They gave birth to several groups of children. These included the Titans, the Cyclopes, and the Centimani.

The Titans were the first true gods. They consisted of six sons and six daughters and several grandchildren are usually included as well. Some of the most notable of the children were Oceanus (world river), Hyperion (the sun), Phoebe (the moon), Iapetus (mortality), and Cronus (time). Important among the grandchildren were Atlas, Prometheus and Epimetheus, all sons of Iapetus, who would later have important dealings with mankind.

The Cyclopes and Centimani were each three sons of monstrous ugliness and strength. The Cyclopes each had a single large eye in the center of their forehead. Their names were Brontes (thunder), Steropes (lightning) and Arges (flash). The Centimani (literally "the hundred–handed") each had one hundred hands and fifty heads and were giants of incredible strength and ferocity.

At the birth of the Cyclopes and Centimani, their father Uranus was repulsed by their ugliness. He imprisoned them in their mother Gaia's body, deep in the earth. This caused Gaia great pain and she cried out to her other sons to help her. Cronus, the youngest Titan, responded to her call for help. He ambushed and defeated his father, Uranus, ending his reign and supplanting him as ultimate ruler of the gods. Cronus did not, however, free his brothers from Gaia's body, but left them imprisoned. As a result, Gaia foretold a day when one of Cronus' own sons would overthrow him.

Zeus and His Brothers

In time, the Titans Cronus and Rhea became husband and wife. Rhea gave birth to six sons and daughters. Because of his treachery when he overthrew his father, Cronus' mother Gaia had prophesied that one of his sons would overthrow him. Each time Rhea gave birth and presented the child to Cronus he would gaze lovingly at it, then suddenly, overcome by a wild madness, he would swallow the baby god or goddess whole.

At the birth of her final son, Zeus, Rhea asked her mother Gaia for help. Gaia told Rhea to take a rock, wrap it in blankets and present it to Cronus as his new son. Rhea did as Gaia bid and when presented with his new son, Cronus mistakenly ate the rock (though he was powerful, he was apparently a little slow). Rhea then sent her newly-born son, Zeus, into hiding in a cave on Mount Ida in Crete to be raised in secret by mountain nymphs.

When Zeus reached adulthood, he set about to free his siblings. He went to his mother, Rhea, and was presented to Cronus as a cupbearer. One day, Zeus slipped an emetic into Cronus wine, causing him to vomit up all the children he had previously swallowed. Because they were immortal gods and goddesses, all were in perfect health and grown to adulthood. Cronus was, understandably, angry and called on his fellow Titans to battle his children. Thus began the Titanomachy, or War with the Titans.

The Titanomachy lasted for ten long years. On one side was Cronus and the other male Titans, elder gods of immense power. On the other was Zeus and his brothers, Poseidon and Hades (who would come to be known as the Olympian gods). Several Titans, most notably Prometheus, also came to their aid. Since Zeus and his brothers were outnumbered, their first act was to free the Cyclopes and Centimani imprisioned deep in the earth. As payment for their release, the Cyclopes made weapons for the Olympian gods; for Zeus the thunderbolt, for Poseidon the trident, and for Hades a cap of invisibility. The Centimani attacked the Titans, throwing rocks as big as mountains, a hundred at a time.

Eventually, the Titans were defeated and imprisoned deep in Tartarus, the underworld, gaurded by their brothers, the Centimani. Zeus and his brothers drew lots to decide who would reign over which parts of the world. To Zeus fell the sky, to Poseidon the oceans, and to Hades the underworld. They made their dwelling high on Mount Olympus in Greece. In this way began the rule of the Olympians.

Olympian Gods

Jupiter

Zeus is the chief god of the Olympians, the sky god (Romans called him Jupiter). Also known as "the thunderer", he is the youngest of the elder Olympians. His weapon is the thunderbolt, forged by the one-eyed Cyclopes. He was well known for his many extra-marital affairs and many of the lesser Olympian gods and goddesses are his children. His animals are the eagle and bull and the oak tree is special to him.

Neptune

Poseidon is god of the seas. He is sometimes called Neptune and is usually depicted with a fish tail, carrying his powerful trident. He is called "earthshaker" and used his trident to cause earthquakes and tsunamis. His animals are the horse and the dolphin. He is father to many children, including the hero Theseus, the giant Orion, and several kings and queens around the Mediterranean Sea.

Pluto

Hades is the god of the underworld. It would be a mistake, however, to consider him death itself; he only oversees the land where the dead reside. His Roman name is Pluto. His weapon is an invisible hat. Living under the earth, he knows the locations of many gems and jewels and so is considered the god of wealth. His animals are Cerberus, the three-headed dog, and any black-colored animals.

Apollo

Apollo is the god of the sun. Each day, he drives his flaming chariot across the sky, pulling the sun along behind him. He is also revered as patron of archery, prophecy, medicine, dance and music. His father is Zeus.

Mercury

Hermes is also a son of Zeus. He was the god of many things, most notably animals, thieves, roads, athletics, medicine, and astronomy. He is the messenger of the gods, being the fastest of them, and usually wears winged sandals wings or a winged hat, and carries a staff with two snakes entwined around it (the Caduceus). His Roman name is Mercury.

Mars

Ares (another son of Zeus) is the god of war or, more correctly, slaughter. His Roman name is Mars. He represents ferocious battle frenzy and careless killing, even of his own side. His weapon is the spear and his animal is the vulture.

Hephaestus is the god of the forge. He is the only crippled god, having been thrown off of Mount Olympus at birth by his father (guess who ... Zeus) because he was ugly. He makes all sorts of mechanical and metal devices for the gods and various heroes, such as Achilles and Hercules. His Roman name is Vulcan. He is often shown riding on a donkey.

Olympian Goddesses

The Greek goddesses are sisters, wives and daughters of the Greek gods. They are mostly related to duties that Greek women would carry out around the home and tended to show the various lifestyles Greek women might live. Some goddesses are married while others remain single for life.

Hera is the wife of Zeus and the goddess of all women. Her Roman name is Juno. She is a very vengeful and jealous goddess. Most of her anger concerns Zeus' many affairs and she spends most of her time watching over him or trying to punish his (many) illegitimate children. Her animals are the peacock and the cow and the pomegranate is her fruit.

Hestia (or Vesta) is one of the three elder Olympian goddesses. She is goddess of the hearth, the fireplace used in all homes for cooking and heating. She is not married. There are not many stories about her, but she is very important in Greek religious and social ceremonies.

Demeter is the third elder goddess. She is also known as Ceres and is goddess of harvests and seasons. Her daughter, Persephone, became the wife of Hades. The pig is her sacred animal.

Athena is a daughter of Zeus. She is the goddess of wisdom. Her animal is the owl. She is also considered the goddess of warfare. She delights in helping mortal heroes, such as Odysseus, Jason, and Hercules. She is said to have jumped out of Zeus' forehead at birth, fully dressed and prepared for battle. The city of Athens is named for her. Her Roman name is Minerva.

Artemis is another daughter of Zeus. Her Roman name is Diana and she is the goddess of the moon and the hunt. Her twin brother is Apollo. Her sacred animal is the deer.

Aphrodite (or Venus) is the goddess of love. She is wife of Haephastus, but only because Zeus commanded it. She is the most beautiful goddess and is usually shown as rising out of the ocean on a shell. Her Roman name is Venus. The dove and swan are her sacred animals.

Persephone is the final important Greek goddess. She is a daughter of Zeus and became the wife of Hades after he kinapped her to his underworld realm. Her mother, Demeter, searched for her many days. Eventually, Demeter found her daughter and demanded that Zeus have her returned. Zeus decided that because Persephone had eaten six pomegranate seeds while in the underworld, she would hence forth spend six months of the year with Hades and the other six months with her mother. This is why we have the seasons of Fall and Winter, when Demeter is sad at her daughter's absence.

Creation of Mankind

Prometheus was the son of Iapetus, one of the original Titans. His name means "forethought" or "one who looks ahead" and Prometheus was, indeed, one of the wisest of all the gods. Because he could see the future, he had sided with Zeus and the Olympians during their war with his brother Titans.

Prometheus made the first people, fashioned out of clay or mud. When they first came alive they were frightened by the world around them and especially by the gigantic gods. But Prometheus calmed them and taught them to speak and how to live. He is often thought of as the guardian of mankind.

Prometheus is known to have safeguarded man when it came time for the gods to choose their portion of all sacrifices. Prometheus hid the meat from the bull in the hide and placed the bones under the fat. Zeus saw the fat and, thinking it contained the meat, chose it as the portion for the gods. Zeus was angry when he discovered that Prometheus had tricked him into choosing worthless bones and giving man the meat from the sacrifices.

Aside from creating men and ensuring they had food, Prometheus also gave us fire. He saw people huddling together for warmth on the cold nights and took pity on them. Prometheus silently crept up to Mount Olympus and stole fire from the gods. He brought it down to mankind in a fennel stalk. Prometheus then taught mankind how to tend the fire and eventually make their own. Slowly, the forbidden knowledge spread until one day, Zeus looked out from Mount Olympus and saw hundreds of small fires glowing in the night. He knew at once that mankind had received the secret of fire and knew that only Prometheus would dare defy him in this way.

As punishment for stealing fire (and other offenses against Zeus), Prometheus was chained to a rock high in the Caucasian Mountains. Hephaestus fashioned unbreakable chains to hold the mighty Titan. Each day an eagle would fly to Prometheus and using its beak and talons, eat out his liver. Each night the liver would grow back again. This was Zeus' revenge. Prometheus lay bound to the rock for many years, but he knew that one day a certain hero would come to his rescue and use his herculean strength to break the chains that bound him.

Pandora's Box

While Prometheus, god of forethought, created men, his brother, Epimetheus, god of afterthought (or foolishness), is involved with the first woman.

Zeus was angry with mankind for receiving Prometheus' stolen gift of fire, so he instructed Hephaestus, blacksmith of the gods, to fashion a woman. Hephaestus set to his work with passion, fashioning her from earth and water. All the gods and goddesses gave her gifts: Aphrodite gave her beauty and Apollo musical ability. Hera, at Zeus' command, gave her the gift of curiosity. Last, Zeus himself gave her a beautiful, large storage jar or box that she was told never to open. Because of these gifts, she is given the name Pandora, meaning "all-gifted".

After her creation, Pandora was presented as a bride to Epimetheus, the foolish younger brother of Prometheus. The two fell in love and began living life together on earth. Their daughter was Pyrrha (fire), the first-born human child.

After a time, however, Zeus sent Hermes to call Epimetheus away to a meeting of all the gods. Pandora was left alone for a great time. Though she tried to occupy herself with household duties, she found her thoughts drawn to the gift of Zeus, the box she was not to open. Long she fought against its temptation, but she was eventually overcome by her curiosity and lifted the lid ever so slightly to see what was inside.

Immediately the room was filled with swirling, howling spirits. They were all kinds of evil, sent by Zeus to plague mankind. Hate and hypocrisy, fear and starvation, sickness and death, all escaped the box in a second and went soaring out of the room to the world beyond. Realizing what was happening, Pandora cried out and slammed the lid back into place. But she was too late. Only one thing remained in the bottom of the box – hope, a single blessing that could help mankind overcome the evils that were released.

Twelve Labors of Hercules

Hercules (or Heracles in Greek) is the son of Zeus and a mortal woman. Because he was a half-god, he was born with incredible strength. Because he was Zeus' illegitimate son, his step-mother Hera was very jealous and tried to kill Hercules when he was a baby. She sent two serpents to bite him in his crib, but baby Hercules used his great strength to strangle the snakes before they could strike.

Hercules grew into adulthood, married and started a family. Sadly, Hera would not leave him alone and eventually succeeded in driving Hercules mad. Out of control in this fit of madness, he couldn't tell right from wrong and ended up destroying everything in his own house, including his family.

Overcome with grief Hercules asked the Delphic Oracle what he could do to regain his lost honor. He was told that he must place himself in the service of Eurystheus, King of Mycenae for twelve years. Unfortunately, Hera had co-opted Eurystheus and convinced him to assign Hercules tasks which would lead to his death. These are his Twelve Labors.

1) "Kill the Nemean lion." This lion had impenetrable skin that no weapon could harm. Hercules strangled it then used it's own razor-sharp claws to skin it. Henceforth, he wore it's skin as armor in battle.

2) "Kill the Hydra." This was a nine-headed monster which would re-grow any lost heads. Hercules cut off each head, then had his cousin, Iolas, burn each neck with a torch.

3) "Capture the Ceryneian deer." Hercules chased this golden stag through the countryside for months until it finally lay down out of exhaustion. Atremis, the goddess of the hunt, appeared and was ready to shoot Hercules because the deer was sacred to her. He promised to treat it kindly and release it, so Artemis relented and let him return with it.

4) "Kill the giant boar of Erymanthus." Hercules chased this large boar into a snowdrift where it's huge tusks were useless and, of course, dispatched it.

5) "Clean the Augean stables in one day." These were enormous cattle stables that had never been cleaned of all the filth and waste from the cows. Hercules thought about this task for a while, then climbed the nearby hills and used boulders to divert a river so that it ran through the stables and washed the filth away.

6) "Kill the Stymphalian birds." Hercules defeated these carnivorous birds by using a loud rattle to scare them into flying out of their hiding places. He then shot them with arrows.

7) "Bring me the Cretean bull." Basically, Hercules used his great strength to rope it and ride it back.

8) "Capture the mares of Diomedes." To capture these man-eating horses, Hercules visited their master, Diomedes, and knowing how savage and cruel he was, threw him to his own horses. Afterward the horses were very tame and Hercules led them back.

9) "Bring me the Girdle of Hippolyta." Hippolyta was Queen of the Amazons, a warrior-race of women. Hercules sought them out, thinking he would defeat Hippolyta in battle. But when the Queen saw him, she instantly fell in love and willingly gave Hercules her girdle.

10) "Bring me the cattle of Geryon." Geryon was a giant monster with three bodies, six arms and legs, and three heads. Hercules first dispatched two of Geryon's giant helpers, then shot Geryon himself with arrows before leading the cattle back.

11) "I want the golden apples of the Hesperides." These were magic apples that had been given to Zeus and Hera by Gaia on their wedding day. They grew in an unknown garden guarded by several monsters, including a 100-headed dragon. To find them, Hercules went to the Titan Atlas who was holding the world on his back (this was a punishment for fighting against Zeus during the war with the Titans). Atlas told Hercules that he would get the apples for him if Hercules would give him a rest and hold the earth for a while. Hercules agreed and took over the job of supporting the earth. When Atlas returned with the apples he didn't want to take back his punishment. Hercules pretended to give up, then asked Atlas to show him once more the right way to hold the earth. Once Atlas, who was very proud, held the earth to show him, Hercules picked up the golden apples and walked away.

12) "Bring Cerberus to me alive!" Cerberus was the three-headed dog that guarded the underworld. Upon entering the underworld, Hercules found Hades and was told by the god that he could take Cerberus only if he used no weapons to subdue him. Of course, Hercules simply grabbed Cerberus' throats and wrestled the huge dog into submission.

Upon seeing the terrifying monster-dog, Eurystheus was so afraid he told Hercules he would be free from his labors if only he took Cerberus back to Hades. Hercules did and was then free to live out his life, his honor restored.

The Trojan War

The Trojan War was a war fought by the Greeks against the city of Troy. It was such a long and mighty struggle that even the Olympian gods became involved. On the side of the Trojans was Apollo, the sun god, and Ares, the frightening god of war. The Greeks were supported by mighty Poseidon, god of the sea, and Athena, goddess of wisdom.

The war started, so it is said, when Paris, prince of Troy, stole away Helen, wife of the King Menelaus of Sparta, the most beautiful woman in the world. Menelaus and his brother, King Agamemnon called all the Greeks together and launched a huge fleet of boats to attack the city of Troy. Thus it is said that Helen had "a face that launched a thousand ships".

The War itself lasted ten long years. The first year alone was spent sailing to Troy through several dangers and missteps. During the next nine years many heroic warriors fell on both sides of the conflict. Mighty Hector, prince of Troy, was defeated in battle by the matchless Greek warrior Achilles. Achilles' mother had dipped him in the underworld river Styx as a child, so he was invulnerable to harm. Unfortunately, she held him by his heel and when Apollo shared this weakness with Paris, he shot Achilles in the foot with an arrow, killing him instantly.

In the end, it was the cunning of Odysseus that won the battle for the Greeks. He talked the other Greeks into building a huge wooden horse, hiding as many warriors as possible inside of it, then sending the rest of the fleet sailing away as if in retreat.

The Trojan warriors came out of their fortified city and seeing the magnificent wooden statue, thought it was a parting gift from the Greeks. They rolled it into their city and held a celebration party that night. When all the Trojan warriors were asleep, the Greeks within the horse quietly snuck out and slaughtered all the Trojans as they slept. King Menelaus recovered Helen and sailed for home. Thus ended the great Trojan War.

The Odyssey

The Odyssey is a story written by the poet Homer that takes up the fate of Odysseus (or Ulysses), hero of the Trojan War, as he strived to return to his home in Ithaca. Odysseus was known for his wisdom and strategies. He was the one who thought up the ruse of the Trojan Horse by which the great battle was finally won. His problems begin when he boasts to the god Poseidon of his own great wisdom and in response, Poseidon blows Odysseus' ship so far off course that it takes ten years for him to return to his home.

The first place Odysseus and his men reach is the island of Calypso, a magical nymph who falls in love with Odysseus. She keeps him and his men captive for seven years. Eventually, Hermes, messenger of the gods, arrives and tells Calypso that Zeus wants her to let Odysseus go. Sadly, she agrees and he and his men set sail.

They next dropped anchor in a sheltered bay at a lonely island. Odysseus led his men on a search for food and fresh water. As they explored the island, they came upon a large cave in the side of a hill. Finding the cave unattended but stocked with food of every type, they rely on the law of hospitality and fall to, eating a good portion of the provisions. As darkness fell, they heard the bleating of sheep and stood up to introduce themselves to their unknown hosts. Their expectation turned to terror, though, as behind the sheep stomped a cyclops, a giant with one eye in the middle of his forehead. He rolled a huge boulder across the exit so the sheep could not escape in the night.

The cyclops, a son of Poseidon whose name was Polyphemus, was more than mildly upset to find that so much of his food had been eaten, so he planned to replace his food by eating Odysseus and his men in the morning. Odysseus hatched a plan to trick him. First, he introduced himself as "Nobody". Then he gave the cyclops all of the wine he and his men had brought with them. As he talked with Polyphemus he had one of his men play a quiet song on his flute while the rest sharpened a log with their swords and heated it in the fire. Soon, Polyphemus was nodding off to a snoring sleep. Then, as the flute-player kept up his lullaby, they plunged the sharpened log into the cyclops' eye, blinding him.

Polyphemus woke, blindly groping about for his attackers. He moved the boulder from the mouth of the cave, calling to his brothers for help. As Polyphemus waited at the cave exit, Odysseus herded the sheep out and had his men hang from their bellies. Polyphemus felt the sheep's wool and the men escaped. Realizing they had gotten out, Polyphemus rushed to the sea shore and hurled boulders out to sea, missing Odysseus' ship by many yards. "Father", he cried. "Nobody has blinded me! Nobody has escaped!"

Other adventures followed. Odysseus journeyed to the land of the dead to get directions from a prophet. They received a magic bag of wind from Aeolus, god of all winds, who wanted to defy Poseidon. But his men thought the bag conatined a treasure. They waited until Odysseus was asleep, then opened the bag, blowing their ship even farther off course and away from home. Next, their ship landed on the sorceress Circe's island and, after Odysseus convinced her to un-transform his men from pigs, they stayed for a year. Upon leaving, they had to naviga te past both Scylla, a many-headed dagon-like monster that hid in caves, and Charybdis, a bottomless whirlpool that tried to suck them down. When they came upon the beautiful, but deadly Sirens, Odysseus had his men put wax in their own ears, but tied himself to the mast so he could hear the song.

Finally, after ten years of traveling, Odysseus reached the shore of his homeland, Ithaca. Athena, the goddess of wisdom, appeared and gave him advice. Suitors, Athena said, had infested his home these past ten years, all trying to marry his supposed widow, Penelope. His wife had refused as long as possible, even stalling by knitting a funeral blanket and unraveling it each night. Eventually, when her son, Telemachus, had grown old enough to have a beard, she decided she could stall no more. She promised the suitors that she would marry whichever of them could string her late husband's mighty war bow and then match his famous archery skill by shooting an arrow through twelve axe handles. Athena then magically disguised Odysseus as an old man and he entered his home as a beggar.

As the contest began, Odysseus enlisted the help of his son, who recognized him. They locked all the doors to the hall and removed all weapons, save their own. Time past as each suitor tried and failed to string the huge bow. Odysseus, still disguised as an old beggar stepped forth and with a twist of his wrist and bend of his mighty back, notched the bowstring. Then, to the amazement of the suitors, he knelt down and sent a single arrow whistling through the handles of the axes. As they gaped in astonishment, the disguise fell away and Odysseus stood revealed. Angered that they had tried to steal his life, Odysseus and Telemachus attacked, quickly dispatching all of the suitors. Finally, Odysseus was reunited with his wife and returned to his throne. He was back where he was meant to be.

Jason and the Argonauts

Jason, the son of Aeson and Alcimede, was the rightful heir to the throne of Thessaly. But because his evil uncle Pelias was killing off all of Aeson's relatives, Jason was sent into hiding with the wise centaur Chiron. Eventually, Pelias became king, but was told by an oracle that he should fear the man wearing only one sandal. Far away from the capital city of Iolcus, Jason grew to manhood.

Years later, King Pelias held athletic games in honor of the god Poseidon. Jason journeyed to Iolcus, losing a sandal as he helped an old woman cross a river. When he revealed himself to his uncle, Pelias promised to give up his throne if Jason would bring the Golden Fleece back to Thessaly.

To find the Golden Fleece, Jason assembled a great group of heroes. They were called the Argonauts, after the name of their mighty ship, the *Argo*. The heroes included the mighty Hercules, the archer Philoctetes, Peleus the father of Achilles, the incredible musician Orpheus, the warlike twins Castor and Pollux, the great athlete Atalanta, and Euphemus who could walk on water.

One of their first stops was to find Phineus, the blind oracle. He agreed to tell them where the Golden Fleece was if they would kill the Harpies. These were ugly bird-women who attacked Phineus each day to stop him from eating. The Argonauts agreed and after dispatching the Harpies, were told how to get to Colchis, the land of the Golden Fleece.

On the way to Colchis, the *Argo* had to pass between two huge clashing rocks. Phineus had told Jason to release a dove and after the rocks came together, row with all their might. The dove made it through, the rocks began to separate and the crew rowed for their lives, barely making it through.

When they arrived in Colchis, King Aeetes agreed to let Jason have the Golden Fleece if he performed a series of tasks. Jason was told he had to yolk a team of fire-breathing oxen, plow a field with them, and sow the field with dragon's teeth. If he survived that, he had to get past the dragon which guarded the Golden Fleece. In all of these tasks, Jason had the secret help of King Aeete's young daughter, the sorceress

Medea, who had fallen in love with him. She gave him an ointment to protect him from the fiery breath of the oxen. Then Medea told him that the dragon's teeth would sprout up as warriors and attack him. To survive, Jason threw a rock into their midst and, not knowing who had thrown it, the warriors attacked each other. Finally, Medea gave Jason a potion to make the dragon fall asleep while he stole the Golden Fleece.

Knowing King Aeetes would not be happy, Jason and the Argonauts sailed away immediately, taking Medea with them. When King Aeetes learned of this, he followed with his navy. To save her new love, Medea killed her own brother and threw him overboard so that her father would stop chasing them.

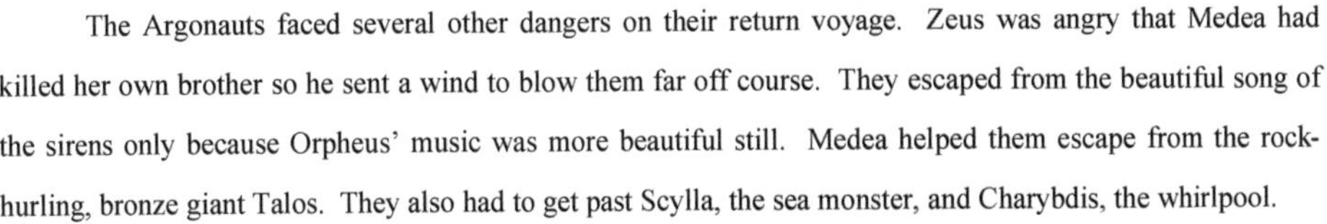

The Argonauts faced several other dangers on their return voyage. Zeus was angry that Medea had killed her own brother so he sent a wind to blow them far off course. They escaped from the beautiful song of the sirens only because Orpheus' music was more beautiful still. Medea helped them escape from the rock-hurling, bronze giant Talos. They also had to get past Scylla, the sea monster, and Charybdis, the whirlpool.

Finally, the Argonauts returned to Thessaly with the Golden Fleece. Medea again helped Jason by getting rid of the treacherous King Pileas. She told his daughters that she could make their father young again if they chopped him up in boiling water and she added a magic herb. The daughters carried out their part of the plan, but Medea refused to add the magic herb, so Pileas remained dead. Because of this evil deed, she and Jason were forced to flee to Corinth.

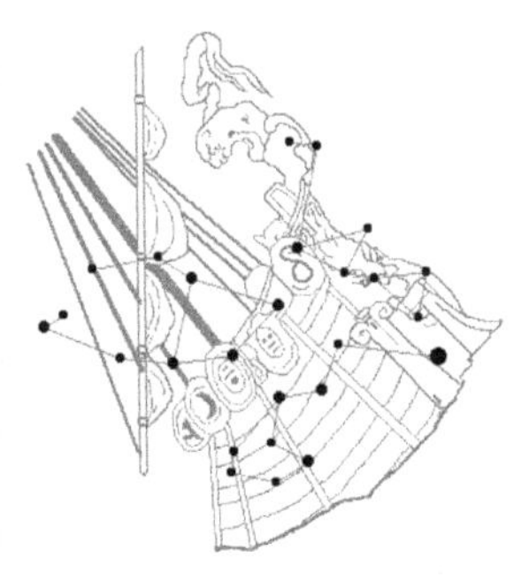

The rest of Jason's life was shrouded in misery. He and Medea eventually split up, some say because of he fell in love with another woman. Jason lived out his life alone until one day, as he was sitting beneath the prow of the *Argo*, a rotting timber broke loose and fell on him, ending his life. In honor of Jason's heroic voyage, Zeus took the *Argo* and lifted it up into the sky, creating the constellation Argo for all to see for all time.

Perseus and Medusa

Perseus is a famous hero in Greek mythology. He is known for killing the gorgon Medusa and saving the beautiful Andromeda. He is also reputed to have founded the Greek city Mycenae.

Perseus was the son of Danae, a mortal woman, and Zeus. Danae's child was destined to kill her father, King Acrisius. Once he found out that Danae had her child, the king set them afloat in a wooden chest in the ocean. The gods heard their prayers for help and when the chest washed ashore on an island, the fisherman Dictys took them in and cared for them.

After Perseus was grown to manhood, the king of the island sent him off on a heroic journey, to slay the monster Medusa. Medusa had been a beautiful woman, but a vengeful goddess changed her into a hideous monster whose look would turn anyone to stone. Perseus, of course, needed godly help. Hermes gave him winged sandals, Athena gave him a bronze shield, and Hades gave him a hat of invisibility. Perseus flew to Medusa's lair with the winged sandals, used the hat of invisibility to sneak up on her, all the while looking at her reflection in the bronze shield so he would not be turned into stone. Then he chopped off her head, stuck it in a bag and headed back home.

On the way home, he showed Medusa's head to the Titan Atlas, turning him to stone and creating the Atlas Mountains. He also used it to save the beautiful Andromeda from a sea monster. Finally, Perseus returned to his island home and used Medusa's head to depose the king who had sent him on the quest.

Perseus returned the magical weapons to the gods who had gifted them. To Athena he also gave Medusa's head. She had it placed on her shield which she used in battle.

One day, Perseus returned to his mother's homeland for an athletic competition. As he was throwing the discus, it slipped from his fingers. Tragically, it struck his grandfather, King Acrisius, in the head, killing him and completing the ancient prophecy.

Theseus and the Minotaur

Theseus was a famous Greek hero, most widely known for defeating the minotaur. He is most closely associated with the city-state of Athens.

When Theseus was born, his father, Aegeus, left to become king of Athens. He had buried his sandals and sword under a rock, though, and told Theseus' mother when he was man enough, he could move the rock, return the items and claim his birthright. When Theseus was finally old enough and moved the rock, his mother told him the truth about his father and that he could find him in Athens.

Wearing the sandals and holding the sword, Theseus set out on the journey to Athens, where his father was king. Being heroic, he decided to take the land route, which was considered far more dangerous than the water way.

On the way to Athens, he ran into and defeated many miscreants. The first was Periphetes, who would beat travelers with an iron club. Thesus defeated him and took the club, which is why he is often drawn holding a club in his hands. The second villain, Siris, would tie the unwary between two bent-down trees, then let the trees go, tearing them apart. Theseus tricked him, however, and dispatched him by his own method. The next bandit was Sciron, who would force travelers to wash his feet, then kick them off a cliff when they kneeled down. Theseus turned the tables on him, pushing him off the cliff instead. Next, Theseus beat Cercyon in a wrestling match. Finally, Theseus defeated Procrustes, a bandit who would offer travelers a warm bed to sleep in, then stretch them or cut them down to size when they didn't fit.

When Theseus arrived in Athens, he was not immediately recognized by his father. Stories differ as to how his identity came out in the open, but eventually king Aegeus saw the sandals and sword and knew Theseus was his son. Father and son were happily reunited. But Theseus' trials were not over yet.

The Athenians owed a yearly ransom to Minos, king of Crete, because of a war they had recently lost against him. The ransom was seven men and seven women, which were then sacrificed to the monstrous minotaur, a half-man, half-bull creature which lived deep in a maze-like labyrinth. Theseus volunteered to go as one of the youths and slay the minotaur. He promised his father that if he were successful, his returning ship would fly a white sail instead of the usual black sail.

On arriving in Crete, the Athenian youths were relieved of all weapons and sent into the labyrinth. Theseus, however, had the help of king Minos' daughter, Ariadne, who had fallen in love with the hero at first sight. She gave him a ball of string to unroll behind him as he walked through the labyrinth so he could find his way out later. She also told him the secret of the maze given to her by its architect, Daedalus: always forwards, always down, never left or right.

In the heart of the dark labyrinth, Theseus came upon the sleeping minotaur. Holding his breath, he crept as close as possible and launched a lightning-fast strike at its head. Enraged and bellowing in pain, the minotaur leapt to its feet and spun to the attack. There followed a horrific battle that some say lasted for hours. No one knows exactly what pains Theseus endured or how many times he barely escaped the minotaur's sharp horns. Finally, Theseus managed to kill the monster with his bare hands.

After resting a short while, he followed the string back out of the maze. He gathered the other Athenian hostages and Ariadne and quietly set sail back to Athens. Something happened on the way home and Ariadne was lost on an island. We don't know if the fault lies with Theseus or someone else, but Theseus, overcome with grief, forgot to change the black sail to white. His father, King Aegeus, saw the black sail, thought his son had failed, and fell to his death in the sea beneath the Athenian cliffs. (For this reason, we call it the Aegean Sea today.) When Theseus landed, he was (again) overcome with grief, but soon took his rightful place as the new king of Athens.

An interesting philosophical side note from this story is the *Ship of Theseus Paradox.* It seems the ship Theseus returned in was kept as a memorial in Athens for several centuries. As parts of it wore out, they were replaced with new wood, until it was unclear how much of the original ship remained. This led to the question of whether or not it should still be considered "the same" ship. This type of question about the nature of identity became known as the *Ship of Theseus Paradox.*

EGYPTIAN STORIES

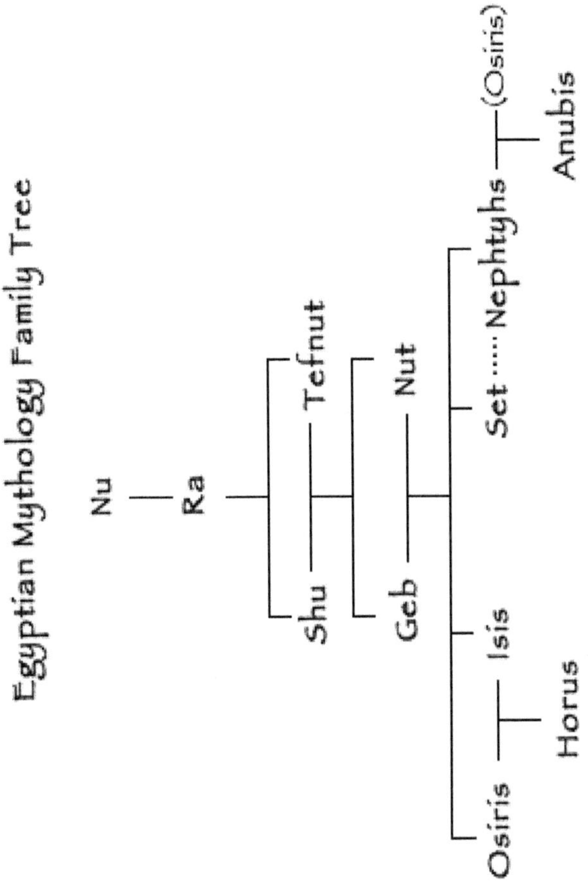

Egyptian Mythology Family Tree

Nu

Ra

Shu — Tefnut

Geb — Nut

Osiris — Isis

Horus

Set ..... Nephtyhs — (Osiris)

Anubis

Egyptian Mythology Stories

Main Egyptian Gods

Many different gods were worshipped in various cities of Egypt during their long kingdom. Sometimes one god's name was combined with another to meld the two into one persona. Of them all, nine were the most agreed upon. These nine were usually called the Pesedjet, or the Ennead in Greek.

Ra was the elder sun god. He is drawn as a man with the head of a falcon and a sun disk over his head. To distinguish him from the later sun gods he is usually shown seated on a throne, as if he were old and tired. Ra is considered by most to be the first Egyptian god to come out of Nu, the primordial chaos.

The other four elder Egyptian gods were Shu and Tefnut and their children, Geb and Nut. Together, these four represented air, moisture, earth and the sky. Shu and Tefnut are shown as humans with animal heads while Geb and Nut are simply the earth and the sky. Their children were the next four gods, Osiris, Isis, Set, and Nephthys.

Osiris was the eldest of the younger Egyptian gods. He was god of the sky at first, but because he died and came back to life, he became the god of the dead. He is shown wrapped as a mummy with a green face.

Isis is the sister and wife of Osiris. She is the goddess of magic, the arts, and nature. She is usually shown with a throne on her head because she ruled in Osiris' place for a while.

Set is considered an evil trickster god. He is the one who killed Osiris and tried to take his throne. Set is shown as a human with the head of a mythical beast called a Typhon. This beast has large ears and a horse-like nose.

Nephthys was the wife of Set, until he killed Osiris, whereupon she left him. She is the goddess of temples and protection. She is also the mother of Anubis, through Osiris.

Minor Egyptian Gods

Anubis is the jackal-headed son of Osiris and Nephthys. He is the god of mummification and protects Egyptian tombs. He is also the one who weighs the souls of the dead in front of Osiris.

Bast is the goddess of music and dancing. She is closely associated with cats and is usually drawn as a woman with a cat's head.

Bes is a dwarf-god, the protector of children and mothers. He was very strong and was shown with a beard.

Hathor is the goddess of love. She is shown as a woman with cow's horns or, sometimes, a cow's head. She is closely associated with Ra.

Horus is the falcon-headed son of Osiris and Isis. He is the youngest sky (or sun) god and fights against his evil uncle, Set.

Ma'at is the goddess of truth and justice and the wife of Thoth. She usually has a single feather above her head. This is the feather against which souls are weighed upon death to determine if they re good or evil.

Ptah is the god of all craftsmen, including architects, metal workers, artists, and builders. He is shown as a mummy with a rounded hat holding a sceptre. His wife is Sekhmet.

Sekhmet is the lion-headed goddess of war. She is called the "eye of Ra" and will sometimes have a sun-disk on her head. She delights in battle and slaughter.

Sobek is a crocodile-headed god. He is god of the Nile and sailors pray to him to protect them from crocodile attacks. He is also associated with crops and food.

Thoth is the god of wisdom and magic. He is shown with the head of an Ibis, a bird with a long, narrow beak. Usually, Thoth is writing something in a book.

The Story of Ra

Ra was the Egyptian sun god and his cult was located in Heliopolis. He was worshiped as the creator and ruler of the world. From times of old, the pharaohs revered Ra and often associated themselves with him, calling themselves the sons of Ra and assumed all of his powers. It was thought that Ra himself sired each pharaoh. He became known as the god of the living, while Osiris was called the god of the dead.

Various tales have different origins of Ra. One claims he came from Nu (the primordial chaos - ocean), another states he rose from an egg, and the third says he came from a lotus flower on the ocean. However he emerged, he then produced all other gods, men, and creatures.

Ra governed his land from a princely palace. Each morning he would set out in his boat and visit the twelve provinces of his kingdom, spending an hour in each one. This came to symbolize the sun's passage in the sky.

Ra took different guises at different times of the day. At night he was a human that wore a double crown. At dawn, he was a sacred beetle and at noon he was a man with the head of a falcon. Some believed that every morning, he was born again as a child and grew during the day into a man. Then in the evening, he would age and die.

When Ra became old and weak, the mortal men began to plot against him. Ra discovered their plots and foiled them, but he was exhausted and greatly disillusioned by all of this. He wished to withdraw from the world so the goddess Nut was ordered by Nun to change herself into a cow and take Ra on her back into the heavens. This placed the sun in the sky and created the world for humans.

Ra and Sekhmet

Ra was the sun-god, King of the gods and creator of all things, including mankind. Long ago, Ra lived on the earth and ruled a glorious kingdom. For a long while this kingdom thrived and men gave Ra the respect due him, but Ra began to grow old and they mocked him. Ra was very angry when he heard the blasphemy of mankind and he gathered the gods to him to hear their counsel.

Ra spoke to the other gods and goddesses: "Hear me! The men that I created have made me angry through their disrespect! But before I destroy them I would listen to your wisdom."

One of the gods answered: "You, oh Ra, are a mightier god than I. Mankind deserves to perish for their lack of respect! Turn your eye upon the men who blaspheme you and they shall perish from the earth." This counsel pleased Ra, so he turned his gaze upon the men of the earth. Fearful of the sun's might, they ran away and hid among shadows where the harsh gaze of the sun could not reach.

Ra again called the gods together. This time they told him to send his eye down among the men so they could not hide. Ra was pleased again by this consel, so he plucked his eye from his head and threw it to the earth. At once, it turned into the fierce lioness Sekhmet, the goddess of war and slaughter. She sought and found hiding places of men, striking fear in their hearts and slaying many of them. She returned that night to Ra, who was satisfied that mankind had begun to respect him again. But having tasted blood, Sekhmet wanted to return and hunt the next day.

Ra realized that Sekhmet would not stop until her bloodthirstiness had destroyed the human race. Angry as he had been, he wished to rule mankind, not utterly destroy it. Again, the other gods came to his aid. They conseled that the only way to stop Sekhmet was to trick her. So Ra ordered his attendants to brew seven thousand jars of alcohol and color it red using some blood, then pour the mixture on the fields. In the morning Sekhmet saw the flooded fields, drank deeply of the mixture (which looked like blood), and eventually fell asleep. When she finally awoke she had changed into the other side of her personality, Hathor, the cow-headed goddess of love. Mankind was saved.

Shu and Tefnut / Geb and Nut

Shu and Tefnut were twin brother and sister. They were the first two gods created by Ra alone. Shu held up the sky and thus became known as the god of air. He was represented as a man with an ostrich feather. Tefnut was shown as a lioness or as a woman with the head of a lion. She was the goddess of rain and dew. Together they represented the space between heaven and earth.

Shu ruled his kingdom wisely and well. When it became time for him to move on, he abdicated his throne, going up to the sky in a mighty storm.

In time, Shu and Tefnut gave birth to Geb (the earth) and Nut (the sky or heavens). Geb is usually seen as a man with the head of a snake. Nut is usually depicted as a woman with stars all over her body stretched out in the sky. Though they were brother and sister, Geb and Nut loved one another greatly.

As time past Geb and Nut became the parents of four other Egyptian gods: Osiris, Isis, Set, and Nephthys. Together, these nine (Ra, Shu, Tefnut, Geb, Nut, Osiris, Isis, Set, and Nephthys) make up the main Egyptian pantheon, often called the Ennead.

This is how Geb and Nut's children were born. When Ra discovered that Geb and Nut had married, he ordered Shu (the air) to come between them and separate them. Nut was rasied high into the sky where she remains to this day, forever gazing down at her far away love, the earth. Ra also commanded that Nut could not bear a child on any day of the year. Thoth, the god of wisdom, (though some stories say it was Khonsu, god of the moon) took pity on Nut and played a game with her allowing her to win five extra days to be added on to the year. (This is why there are 365 days on the official calendar, instead of 360). On these days (often called the Demon Days) Nut was able to give birth to her children.

Geb, like his father Shu, was a wise ruler. When it was time for him to give up his throne, he gladly left it for his son, Osiris, to rule. As we will see, Osiris reign did not go as well as his father's or grandfather's.

Osiris & Isis

Osiris was the first-born son of Geb and Nut. He was born in Thebes in Upper Egypt. His great grandfather Ra willingly accepted him as his heir. He was both handsome and tall, and when Geb retired to the heavens, Osiris succeeded him as king of Egypt and his sister Isis, became his queen.

Osiris immediately set out to improve the quality of life for his subjects. He abolished cannibalism, taught the people how to farm and produce grapes and grains, built towns, established laws, and started the cults for the gods and goddesses by building the first temples and creating statues of them. He also invented the flute, which was considered a religious instrument.

After all of this was completed, he set out on the peaceful conquest of Asia. He left Isis as regent in his absence and took Thoth and Anubis with him. He traveled throughout the world and by music and goodness, he won over many countries. Returning to Egypt, he found that Isis had kept everything in perfect order. Because she ruled in his absence, Isis is usually shown with a throne on her head.

Osiris' return to Egypt upset his brother Set, who was jealous of Osiris' power and success. Where Osiris was popular and handsome, Set was despised and ugly. So Set plotted against Osiris, hoping to seize the throne. Taking advantage of the festivities of Osiris' return, Set invited his brother to a banquet. During the banquet, Set produced a magnificent golden coffin and explained that it would belong to the god who could fit into it. One by one, the gods and goddesses tried fitting into the magnificent coffin, but all were the wrong size.

Finally, against Isis' advice, Osiris agreed to try fitting into the coffin. Slowly he lowered himself into it. It was a perfect fit! At once Set jumped forward and slammed down the lid to the coffin, nailed it closed, carried it away to the nearby Nile River and threw it in! Isis and the other gods tried to save their king, but Set was too powerful. The golden coffin drifted out to sea and came to rest many months later at the foot of a great tamarisk tree in Phoenicia.

The tamarisk tree grew with such speed that it quickly encased the coffin within its trunk. The king of Byblos saw the magnificent tree and ordered it to be cut down and used as a support for his new palace. He was unaware of the coffin inside of the tree, however. When the tree was cut down, it gave off the most marvelous scent and the rumor it spread far and wide. When Isis heard of the tree, she immediately recognized what it meant and quickly traveled to Phonecia. She persuaded the king to give her the tree trunk and freed the coffin from the wood. Then she took it back to Egypt where she hid it in the swamps.

One day soon after, Set was hunting in the swamps and he discovered the coffin that he thought was long lost. He opened it and ordered the body of Osiris to be cut into fourteen pieces and scattered throughout the land. This cruelty angered many of the gods, even Set's wife Nephthys, who left him and joined Isis and her followers.

For a long time, Isis searched for the fourteen pieces of Osiris. She eventually found all of them, except for one. Isis put Osiris back together with linen wrappings and performed the first act of embalming, which restored Osiris to eternal life. Because one of the pieces was missing, however, Osiris could no longer be the pharaoh, or ruler, of the living in Egypt, so he took his place as the god of the dead. His face is shown colored in green to denote that he has died. When her work was done, Isis hid in the swamps to avoid Set and to bring up her son Horus until he was old enough to seek revenge for his father's murder.

The Battle of Set and Horus

Set was the evil brother of Osiris and Isis. When he was born, he was covered with red hair. He was jealous of Osiris and tricked him into a coffin which he threw into the Nile. When it was recovered by Isis, Set had Osiris' body cut into fourteen pieces and scattered throughout the land. This murder angered the other gods and they banished Set to the desert.

Set represented the spirit of evil and destruction and was associated with the arid desert, drought, and darkness. He was cosidered the opposite of Osiris. Such was the anger of the Egyptian people toward Set that the followers of Osiris had Set's name eradicated and all his temples and images destroyed.

Set's animals were the hippopotamus, crocodile, boar, and scorpion. He took the mythical form of a fantastic beast with a thick, curved snout, straight, square ears, and a stiff-forked tail. The Greeks called this creature a typhon.

Osiris and Isis had a child, Horus. He was brought up in secrecy, for fear that his uncle Set would murder him, just like his father. He was a weak child and was saved by a several disasters by his mother's magical powers. Some stories indicate he was bitten by savage beasts, stung by scorpions, burnt, and suffered stomach pains. Later, Horus became associated with cures for these ailments.

When he was grown, he lived with the people of the Nile River Delta and became their ruler. While he was here, Osiris appeared to Horus in a vision and advised him on how to defeat Set. He told Horus ot enlist the help of the god of wisdom and magic, Thoth. Thoth turned Horus into a sun-disk with splendid outstretched wings.

In their first battle, Horus used cunning and deception to win the day. Horus flew up to the sun and flew down to attack Set's armies. Set's generals became confused from staring into the sun trying to see Horus and ordered their troops to attack in the wrong direction. In rage and confusion, Set's army destroyed itself! When the battle was over Horus' enemies were either dead or scattered. Horus looked throughout the battlefield to find his uncle, but Set had disappeared.

The second battle between the two gods was more traditional. Set collected his remaining minions and turned them into crocodiles and hippopotami, strong, vicious animals from the Nile River with thick, protective hides. Horus had his army make iron lances and heavy chains. Horus also asked Thoth to enchant these weapons with words of powerful magic. When the next battle came, many of Set's lieutenants were slain by the magical weapons, but others escaped into the desert. Battles such as these continued for some time, with neither Set nor Horus able to gain a decisive victory.

After one such battle, Horus took a prisoner who looked like Set. He brought him back to the other gods in chains. Ra, the great sun-god, allowed Horus to determine Set's fate. So Horus dragged Set through the dust of the city and cut him into pieces, undoing the dishonor done to his own father, Osiris.

Many believe that the story ends here. But there are other endings as well. In one telling, the other gods decided it was time to make their own judgment and called both Horus and Set before them. After much deliberation, the tribunal decided to condemn Set and make Horus ruler of all of Egypt. Thus, Horus became the national god of Egypt and the ancestor of the pharaohs.

Others say Set was not executed, that he had instead taken the form of a giant snake and hidden himself deep under the desert. Some claim that Ra gave Set to Isis and that it was she who excuted him, not Horus. Still others say that the final battle between Horus and Set never ocurred. When that final battle between good and evil happens, they believe that Horus will be victorious and Osiris and the other elder gods will return to rule the earth once more.

Anubis

Anubis was the god of mummification and the protective deity of cemeteries, credited with the invention of embalming because he helped Isis to preserve her husband Osiris. Osiris' body was the first to be mummified. He is usually shown as a reclining black jackal or a man with a jackal head. The blackness of his face symbolized the rich soil of Egypt and the appearance of a mummified corpse.

Mummification was a complex procedure which involved a series of detailed operations and rituals. To begin with, the body was washed and purified and then the organs were removed. The brain was extracted through the nose using a long metal hook then the left side of the body was opened up to remove the liver, lungs, stomach and intestines. The brains were discarded as worthless, but the heart, which was seen as the seat of all thought, was left in place. The removed organs were washed and dried separately with natron (a type of sodium salt), treated with aromatic oils, and wrapped in linen.

Next the organs were placed into the four Canopic jars. They were called Canopic jars because many of them were found in the Delta port of Canopus. Each jar featured a stopper that looked like a different son of Horus. The jar with a human head held the liver, the baboon-headed jar received the lungs, the jackal-headed jar held the stomach, and the intestines went into the jar with a hawk's head.

After evisceration, the body cavity was washed out and scented and then stuffed with temporary packing which to help dry it out. Natron was also placed over the corpse for forty days. During this stage in the process, the body lost up to seventy-five per cent of its weight. The temporary stuffing would eventually be removed and the body cavity refilled with fresh natron and resin-soaked linen to restore its former shape. Makeup would be used to help the face look realistic.

After being coated in cedar oil and scented resins, the body was wrapped in bandages while priests read out the appropriate incantations from *The Book of the Dead.* High priests often wore an Anubis mask to perform the ceremonial deeds.

At the time of death, Anubis was thought to weigh the heart of the newly dead against the feather symbol of Ma'at, goddess of truth. Horus' four sons (from the Canopic jars) were believed to be present as well. If the heart was not as light as the feather, it meant it was full of evil and the soul was eaten by the crocodile-like goddess, Ammut.

Isis and the Secret of Ra's Name

Isis was the wife of Osiris and the goddess of magic. She also represented the fertile plains of Egypt and was the guardian of travelers. There were festivals and processions in her honor and she also represented the virtues of loyalty, honor, courage, and selflessness. She was pictured with a throne on her head because she ruled Egypt in her husband Osiris' absence. She also has winged arms to protect those who have died because she brought Osiris back to life.

Ra's name in hieroglyphics

The Egyptians were firm believers in magic. The goddess Isis was considered to be especially potent in magical arts and she sometimes used her skills mischievously. One story tells of how she tricked Ra into telling her his secret name of Ra. This gave Isis power over him.

"Isis was a clever woman," explained one story, "more intelligent than countless gods...she was ignorant of nothing in heaven or on earth." She wanted to place herself and her son Horus at the head of the pantheon of gods and the only way to do this was to discover Ra's secret name. One day Isis came upon Ra when he was asleep, snoring loudly. From the corner of his open mouth hung a long dribble of saliva, which gathered weight and fell to the ground.

Isis pounced: scooping up the spittle, she mixed it with clay and made the form of a poisonous snake. Then she breathed magic into the snake to make it come alive. Isis knew that every so often hRae would leave his palace to go for a walk. Each time, on his route, he passed a crossroads. Isis left her snake there and waited.

Ra emerged for his excursion, and - as Isis had planned – when he came to the crossroads, the snake bit him. In pain, he called to the gods of Egypt for help. Ra had a fever and was sweating and shivering, but the other gods were helpless: they could do no more than mourn the impending loss of the god of the sun. Isis then made a dramatic entrance. She could cure Ra, she said, but only if he would tell her his name.

Ra refused. She offered again and again, but still he refused. Eventually his agony became so extreme that he could bear it no longer, and he agreed to give Isis the secret, on condition that she could tell it to no one other than her son, Horus. Isis accepted these terms and speaking aloud the god's true name, she removed the poison. The sun god was cured at once, and Isis attained the power and prestige she had sought for her son.

NORSE STORIES

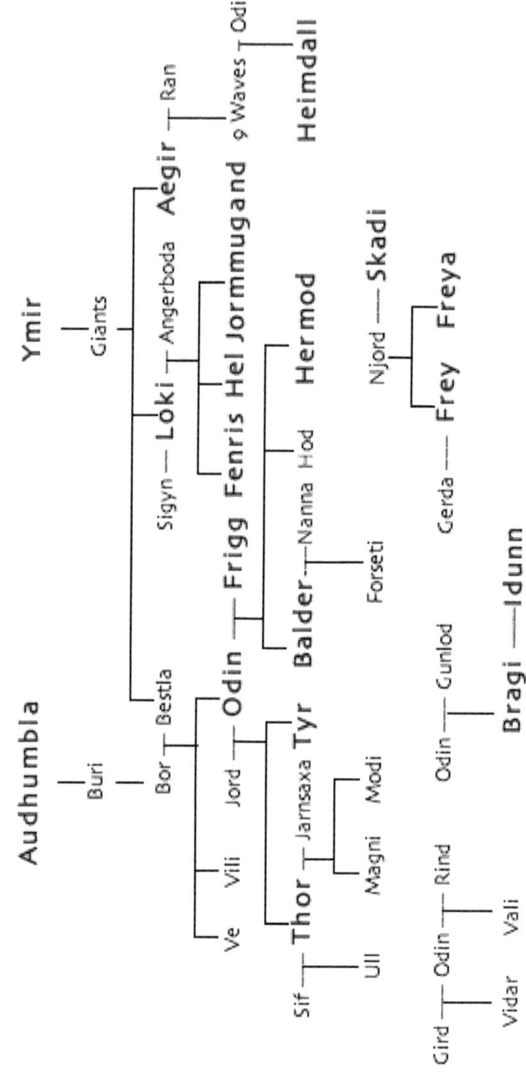
Norse Mythology Family Tree
Audhumbla
Ymir
Buri
Giants
Bor
Bestla
Aegir
Ran
9 Waves
Odin
Heimdall
Ve
Vili
Odin
Sigyn
Loki
Angerboda
Fenris
Hel
Jormmugand
Jord
Frigg
Thor
Tyr
Balder
Nanna
Hod
Hermod
Sif
Jarnsaxa
Ull
Magni
Modi
Forseti
Njord
Skadi
Gerda
Frey
Freya
Gird
Odin
Rind
Vidar
Vali
Odin
Gunlod
Bragi
Idunn

Norse Mythology Stories

Introduction to the Norse Gods

Odin is the leader of the Asgardian gods. He is sometimes called the All-Father. He can be recognized by the patch he wears over one eye, his magical spear, his two ravens and two wolves. He also has a magic horse that can fly. His hall is known as Valhalla, the most beautiful in all of Asgard, where those who died bravely in battle are brought by the Valkyrie (warrior women) to train and fight for the final battle, Ragnarok. Odin is not a god to be trusted by humans, for he may break his word or strike down an ally if it serves his purposes. Odin's wife is Frigg and he has many children. He invented the Runes, the alphabet of the Vikings. Odin's name is sometimes spelled "Woden" and from it we get our word Wednesday.

Thor, the thunder god, Odin's eldest son, is the strongest of gods and men, and possesses three precious things. The most important of these is a magic hammer, named Mjollnir, with which he enjoys killing all manner of giants. He is married to Sif, a light elf. From Thor's name is derived our word Thursday.

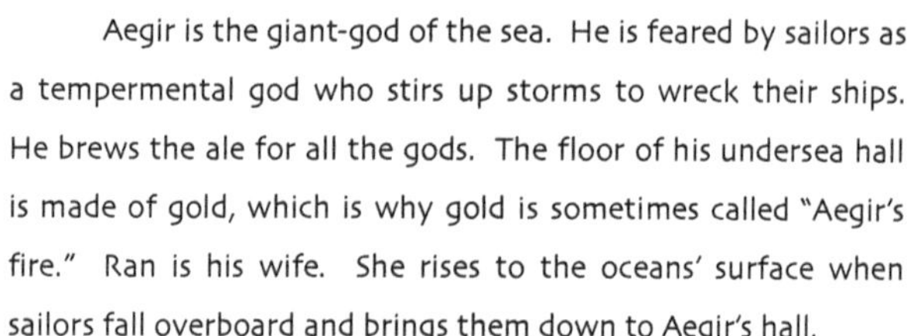

Aegir is the giant-god of the sea. He is feared by sailors as a tempermental god who stirs up storms to wreck their ships. He brews the ale for all the gods. The floor of his undersea hall is made of gold, which is why gold is sometimes called "Aegir's fire." Ran is his wife. She rises to the oceans' surface when sailors fall overboard and brings them down to Aegir's hall.

Frigg is Odin's wife and the goddess of marriage. Her children include Balder, Hod (the blind god), and Hermod, the gods' messenger. It is said she knows the destinies of everyone but will not reveal them. Our day Friday was probably named after her. (Sometimes she is called Frigga.)

Frey, god of the weather, is one of the most celebrated of the gods. He presides over rain, sunshine and all the fruits of the earth. His sister Freya, goddess of love, is the most propitious of the goddesses. She loves music, spring, and flowers, and is particularly fond of the Elves (fairies). She is also very fond of love poems.

Bragi is the god of poetry and his song records the deeds of warriors. His wife, Idunn, the goddess of youth, keeps in a box the golden apples which the gods eat to become young again.

Balder is considered the most handsome of the gods. He is the god of light. His mother, Frigg, made him invulnerable to harm, but he was killed accidentally by his blind brother, Hod. His son is Forseti, god of justice and law. Balder is destined to return to life after Ragnarok, the final battle between the gods and the giants.

Heimdall is the watchman of the gods, and is therefore placed on the borders of heaven to prevent the giants from forcing their way over the bridge Bifrost (rainbow). He requires less sleep than a bird and sees by night as well as by day for a hundred miles around him. So acute is his hearing that no sound escapes him; he can even hear the grass. His father is Odin and his "mothers" are the nine waves, goddess children of Aegir and Ran.

Tyr is the god of war. He is missing his right hand (he lost it to Fenris-wolf). He is a son of Odin and brother to Thor. We get our name for Tuesday from him.

There is another deity who is described as the trickster of the gods and the contriver of all fraud, evil, and mischief. His name is Loki. He is handsome and well made, but of a very fickle mood and most evil disposition. He is of the giant race, but was adopted as a son by Odin. Loki seems to take pleasure in bringing difficulties upon the gods.

Loki has three children. The first is the wolf Fenris, the second the Midgard serpent Jormuggand, and the third Hel (the goddess of death). The gods were not ignorant that these monsters were growing up and that they would one day bring about much evil. When they were brought before Odin, he immediately threw the serpent Jormmugand into the deep ocean that surrounds the earth. But the monster had grown to such an enormous size that he encircles the whole earth. Odin cast Hel into Niffleheim and gave her power over all who die of sickness or old age in the nine worlds. She may easily be recognized, for her body is half white and half black.

Norse Creation

According to the old tales a man with the name of Gylfe, king of Svithiod, once entered the home of the gods and there he was told how the world begun. He met with three beings: Hög (High), Tredje (Third) and Jämnhög (Even Height or something like that). They told him how the world had been created.

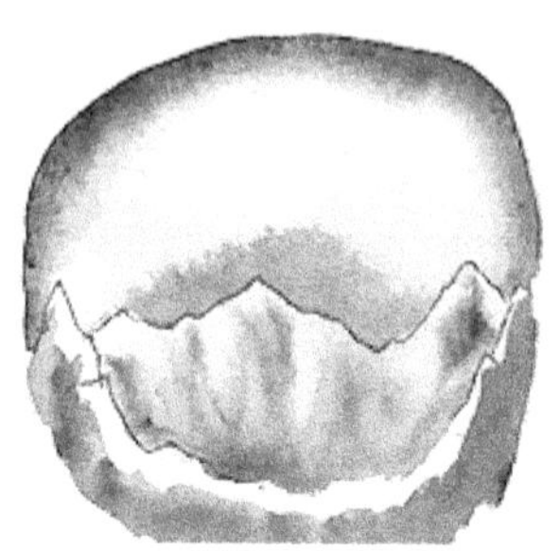

In the beginning there was a deep abyss called Ginnungagap. On one side there was Nifelheim, the world of cold and darkness. Frosty mists rose from Nifelheim into Ginnungagap, filling it with ice. On the other side there was hot Muspelheim, a place of flame. Flares from Muspelheim fell into the abyss and the falling drops of flares and ice formed two giant beings: A cow with the name 'Audhumbla' and a frost giant named 'Ymer'. Ymer got his food from milking the cow. Audhumbla lived by licking frost and salt from the ice.

Ymer created several different creatures. While he slept, a male and female giant grew from his armpits , a six-headed troll from one leg, and a three-headed monster from the other leg. He was the father of the frost and fire giants.

While Audhumbla was licking the ice there appeared on the first day the hair of a man, on the second day the whole head, and on the third the entire form. This new being was Buri, the first god. Buri and his wife, a giantess, had a son name Bor who married Bestla, the daughter of another giant. Bor and Bestla had three sons, Odin, Vili, and Ve.

Ymir was not content with the world as it was. He grew larger and angrier and more evil by the day. The three young gods (Odin, Vili, and Ve) were forced to band together and kill the great menace. Ever since that time there has been hatred and enmity between the gods and the giants.

Odin and his brothers dragged Ymir's body into the void. His flesh became the earth and his blood the sea. His bones became the mountains, his hair the trees, and his teeth the stones. They took Ymir's eyebrows and created the world of Midgard (Earth).

Odin and his brothers discovered worms living in what had been Ymir's body. They turned these into the dwarves and dark elves that beings reside in the depths of the earth, mining the ore and minerals beneath the mountains and hills. The world of the dwarves is known as Nithavellir and the world of the dark elves is called Svartalfheim.

Odin and his brothers also discovered some fine creatures living in the soil formed from Ymir's body. They named these creatures light elves and placed them in the world known as Alfheim. As Ymir's blood flowed, it created a flood that killed all the giants, save one. Bergelmir made his escape with his household in the first boat, a hollowed out tree-trunk.

The sons of Bor then took Ymir's skull and fashioned from it the sky and set it over the earth. Under each corner they placed a dwarf and it is from the names of these dwarves that we get the directions: North, South, East and West. The sons of Bor then took the sparks and burning embers that were flying about and cast them into the midst of Ginnungagap to light the heavens and the earth, creating all the stars and planets.

Next the three gods created night and day. The sun and the moon can never pause in their journey through the sky because they are constantly pursued by two wolves, Skoll and Hati.

One day while Odin and his brothers were walking along the seashore they came upon two tree trunks. The gods saw great beauty in the trunks and set forth to bring them to life. Odin gave them life and soul, Vili gave motion and reason, and Ve gave them senses and speech. These beings were the first humans and they were called Ask and Embla. Midgard was given to them to inhabit and they became the progenitors of the human race.

Order of Worlds in the Universe

Now that the earth was made and had been filled with all manner of beings, the gods created a home for themselves. The gods built for themselves a stronghold known as Asgard. They built a bridge to connect Asgard and Midgard called Bifrost. Asgard is sheltered by the great world tree, Yggdrasil, which touches upon all worlds.

The mighty ash tree Yggdrasill supported the whole universe. It sprang from the body of Ymir and had three immense roots; one extending into Asgard (the dwelling of the gods), the other into Jotunheim (the abode of the giants), and the third to Niflheim (the region of darkness and cold). By the side of each of these roots is a spring, from which it is watered. The root that extends into Asgard is carefully tended by the three Norns, goddesses of fate. They are Urdur (the past), Verdandi (the present), Skuld (the future). The spring at the Jotunheim side is Mimir's well, in which wisdom and wit lie hidden. Odin once gave his right eye for a drink of the water in this well. The well or spring found in Niflheim feeds the serpent Nidhogge (darkness), which perpetually gnaws at the root of Yggdrasil. What is left of Ymir (which isn't much!) lies under the tree and when he tries to shake off its weight the earth quakes.

There are three levels in Norse mythology, in which nine worlds reside:

Upper level

- * Asgard (Aesir – warrior / ruler gods)
- Alfheim (elves)
- Vanaheim (Vanir – produce / fertility gods)

Middle Level

- Midgard (men)
- * Jotunheim (giants)
- Svartalfaheim (dark-elves)
- Nithavellir (dwarves)

Lower Level

- Muspelheim (fire; a flaming, hot world)
- * Niflheim (the dead, the lowest level)

(* indicates where the roots of Yggdrasil are watered at wells)

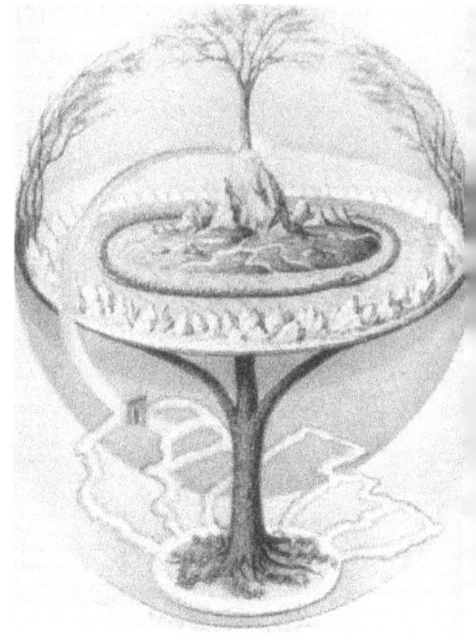

Odin's Thirst for Knowledge

If knowledge is power, secret knowledge is secret power. Odin, the most powerful of the Norse gods, constantly tried to find a way to circumvent Ragnarok, the coming destruction of the gods and the world that he had helped to create. Odin learned from the Norns (goddesses of fate) that he would lead the gods in this final battle against the frost-giants. Few gods will escape this death and destruction. Since Odin was one of those doomed to die, he was obsessed with Ragnarok.

Odin would try anything to gain knowledge. He often resorted to deception, betrayal and murder. Odin was known as the breaker of oaths, since he would break his vows, especially if he could gain advantages from it. Odin also tried to gain knowledge and power by speaking to wise people, such as seers, prophets, and kings.

One way Odin received secret knowledge was by drinking from the well of knowledge. This was near one of the three roots of Yggdrasill, the world tree. It was guarded by the giant Mimir. Mimir was wise because he frequently drank from the well. The price of drinking from the well was not small. Odin gave up one of his eyes so he could drink from it. Heimdall, guardian of Bifrost (Rainbow Bridge) in Asgard, similarly sacrificed a body part to drink from the well, although he only gave up one of his earlobes.

Another way in which Odin learned secret knowledge was by hanging for nine days and nine nights on Yggdrasil. By doing this, he learned to read the rune language.

Odin did have more normal means of gaining news from around the world. One of them comes from his two ravens – Hugin ("Thought") and Munin ("Memory"). These two birds would fly throughout the world each day. When they returned to Valhalla, they gave Odin news of what was happening around the world. The throne itself was also magical and allowed Odin to see certain things that were happening far away. His wife, Frigga, was also said to know the fate of every being, but as she was not allowed to reveal to anyone their future, this didn't help Odin very much.

Gifts of the Dwarves

Thor was married to Sif, a light elf, who had beautiful, long golden hair. It was something in which she took great pride. Loki, the mischievous giant-god, loved playing practical jokes on the gods. One night, Loki decided to cut off all of Sif's hair. What Loki didn't count on, was Thor's temper. When Thor found his wife weeping over the loss of her golden hair, the thunder-god caught Loki and threatened to beat and break every bone in his body. Loki promised Thor that he would replace Sif's beautiful hair with hair of gold.

Loki went to the land of the dwarves (Nithavellir) and sought the master dwarven craftsmen, the sons of Ivaldi. They made him a wig out of finely spun gold. The magical property of the gold hair was that it was alive like real hair and would grow naturally.

The sons of Ivaldi also created two other splendid gifts for the gods. They created the indestructible never-missing spear, called Gungnir, for Odin. They also created a magical ship for Frey, which was called Skidbladnir. Skidbladnir could fly and was a collapsible ship that Frey could fold up and carry in his pocket.

As Loki carried the gifts to the gods, he encountered two other dwarfs – Brokk and Eiti. Loki boasted of the gifts and craftsmanship of the sons of Ivaldi. He made a wager on his life that Brokk and Eiti and could not better the three gifts of the sons of Ivaldi. The two dwarves agreed to the wager.

First, Eiti placed a pig's hide in the forge and told his brother to keep working on the bellows, until he completed the work. As they started working, a fly (Loki?) tried to distract Brokk from blowing air into the forge fire by biting into his left arm. Brokk ignored the fly and continuously worked on the bellows. From the hide, bristles of gold sprouted out and a live wild boar lept from the fire. The boar was called Gullinbursti, "golden bristles" and had the ability to run faster than any horse, across the sky or over water. The gold bristles ensured that it could see where it was going, even in the dark.

During the second piece of work, the fly landed on Brokk's neck, nibbling harder than before, but Brokk ignored the fly and kept working on the bellows. Eiti made a gold ring called the Draupnir. The ring had the ability to make eight other rings of the same size, every nine nights.

While they started working on a third item, the fly landed between Brokk's eyes, and nibbled on his eyelid. Blood dripped into his eye, so Brokk quickly rubbed the blood out of his eye and swatted the fly away before he continued to work the bellows. Eiti had placed a large piece of iron in the forge and together, the two dwarves created the great hammer, Mjollnir. Mjollnir was the strongest weapon in the world. It would not fail to hit any target it was struck or thrown at. If the hammer were thrown, it would always return to its owner, like a boomerang.

Brokk and Loki returned with all the gifts to Asgard. There, Odin, Thor and Frey acted as judges over the gifts, to see which was the best of them all.

First, Loki gave the hair of gold to Sif, to appease Thor's anger towards him. The collapsible ship (Skidbladnir), was given to Frey, and Loki gave the irresistible spear (Gungnir) to Odin. Brokk gave the boar with golden bristles (Gullinbursti) to Frey, the gold ring (Draupnir) to Odin, and the hammer (Mjollnir) to Thor. The three judges found that Mjollnir was the best gift, since it gave them greatest chance to defeat the giants at Ragnarok.

Since Loki lost his wager he tried to flee, but was caught by Thor. Odin decided that Loki losing his head was a bit drastic, so Brokk agreed to a different punishment and sealed Loki's mouth shut for a while.

Death of Balder

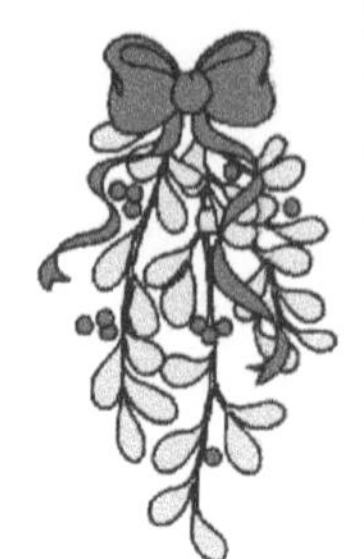

This story begins when Balder, god of light, had some terrible dreams. In these dreams Balder saw his own death. The gods were gathered and Balder shared his dreams with them. When the gods heard these dreams they took counsel and it was decided to seek protection for Balder. Frigg, his mother, went out and gathered an oath from every peril. She received an oath from fire and water, iron and all kinds of metals, stones, earth, trees, ailments, beasts, birds, poison and serpents. All promised that they would not harm Balder.

From this time on, the gods would amuse themselves by striking at Balder with all manner of weapons. Some threw darts, others struck him with weapons and still others threw stones. No matter what was done, Balder remained free from harm. When Loki saw this it upset him. He went disguised as a woman to visit Frigg. He tricked Frigg into telling how Balder had been made invulnerable. The woman (Loki) asked if everything had sworn the oath and Frigg responded that all things save one had given the oath. She said west of Valhalla grew a little bush known as mistletoe which was so small, she thought it unable to bring harm. After hearing this, the woman (Loki) disappeared.

Loki took hold of the mistletoe and carried it to the assembly. There he saw all the gods striking at Balder, save one. This one was Hod, Balder's brother. Loki asked Hod why he wasn't showing Balder honor and throwing darts at him. Hod replied that it was because he was blind and he had no weapon. Loki said, "I will show you where he is standing and you can throw this twig at him". Hod took the mistletoe and, with Loki's guidance, aimed at Balder. Hod then drew back the mistletoe and flung it at Balder. The dart pierced Balder's skin and he immediately fell to the ground, dead.

When Balder had fallen dead, the gods were struck dumb and were unable to move a finger to lift him up. They would have slain Hod where he stood, but ancient laws forbade the shedding of blood in the hall. Hod left, alone and weeping.

When the Gods did try to speak, they wept, and none could tell the others his grief in words. Odin was the most affected by this disaster, for he best understood what a loss the death of Balder was for the gods. When the gods had recovered Frigg was the first to speak. She asked which of the gods wished to win her affection and favor by journeying to Hel to offer a ransom to allow Balder to return to Asgard.

Hermod stepped forward and volunteered to journey to Hel to attempt to ransom Balder back to Asgard. Sleipnir was brought forth and Hermod mounted the steed and galloped away.

Balder's body was carried by the gods to the shore of the sea and was laid upon a ship. The gods wished to launch the ship and build Balder's funeral pyre upon it, but they were unable to move the ship. They sent out a call to Jotunheim for the ogress Hyrrokkin. When she arrived, riding a wolf and using vipers as reins, she jumped off her steed and Odin called for four berserkers to guard her horse. Hyrrokkin went to the prow of the ship and at the first shove launched it into the sea.

Then Balder's body was carried out on to the ship, and when Nanna, Balder's wife, saw that, her heart broke from the grief and she died. Her body was carried on to the pyre and the pyre was set aflame. Thor stepped foward and was consecrating the funeral with Mjollnir when a dwarf, Lit, ran foward. Thor, being hot-tempered and extremely saddened by Balder's death, kicked the dwarf into the fire where he burned to ashes along with Balder and Nanna.

All manner of people came to the funeral. Odin was accompanied by Frigg, the Valkyries and his ravens. Frey drove in a chariot drawn by Gullinbrusti, Heimdall rode Gulltop, and Freya arrived behind her cats. A great crowd of ogres and giants also came to witness the pyre for Balder. Odin came forward and laid the great ring Draupnir upon the pyre.

While these things were taking place, Hermod was riding down to Hel. For nine nights he rode until he came to the river Gjoll and rode across its bridge.

Hermod rode on until he came to the gates of Hel. Hermod dismounted, tightened the stirrups on Sleipnir, remounted and dug his spurs. Sleipnir jumped over the gate with such energy that he came no where near the gate. Hermod then rode up to Hel's hall and dismounted. Inside, he saw Balder sitting at the high seat there. Hermod stayed that night in Niflheim and in the morning he asked Hel if Balder might be allowed to ride home with him. Hermod told Hel how all the gods wept for Balder.

Hel said that a test should be made as to whether Balder was loved as much asHermod claimed. If all things in the world, both dead or alive, would weep for Balder then he would be allowed to return to the gods, but if anyone objected or refused to weep he would have to remain in Niflheim. Hermod stood up and Balder led him out of the hall. Balder took off Draupnir and sent it back to Odin in remembrance. Hermod rode back to Asgard and related all that had transpired.

Upon hearing his message the Gods sent messengers throughout the worlds to ask for tears to weep Balder out of Niflheim. Everywhere they went, the messengers were met with tears--men and beasts, stones and trees, all metals and even the earth--all these things wept for Balder. When the messengers were returning from their journey they met with a giantess, Thokk, sitting in a cave. They asked her to weep for Balder so that he would be released from Hel, but Thokk refused. Some think the giantess was Loki in disguise. Regardless of who it was, because Thokk refused to weep, Balder was resigned to remain in Hel and he will remain there until after the time of Ragnarok.

Fenris' Binding

Fenris was a wolf, the offspring of the giant-god Loki and the giantess Angerboda. His brother was the serpent Jormmugand and his sister was Hel. He was raised in Asgard by the gods where they could watch over him, but he grew so large that the gods became afraid of him. Only Tyr, the god of war, was brave enough to feed and take care of Fenris. Eventually, the gods decided they had to bind him for their safety.

The gods crafted the strongest iron chain known and attached it to Fenris, but he easily broke it. The gods then crafted a second chain, twice as strong as the first and again Fenris struggled and shook until the chain flew apart. At this, the gods sent Skirnir, Frey's messenger, to the dwarves to get them to craft a chain able to hold Fenris.

The dwarves fashioned a bond out of six magical things: the sound of a cat's footfalls, the beard of a maiden, the roots of a mountain, the dreams of a bear, the breath of a fish and the spittle of a bird. When finished,the six strands were were as smooth and thin as silk. The bond they fashioned was called Gleipnir.

The gods brought this silken bond before Fenris told him if it held him fast, they would have no reason to fear him and would release him. Wary of treachery and aware that there was likely some magic in the silken bond, Fenris said he would agree only if one of the gods would place a hand in his mouth as a sign of goodwill. The gods hesitated, but Tyr stepped forward and placed his right hand between the wolf's jaws.

The gods fastened Gleipnir to Fenris and he attempted to break free. As he struggled to free himself, the bond only got tighter. When he realized he could not break free and when the gods refused to release him, he closed his jaw and bit off Tyr's right hand. Realizing Fenris was truly bound the gods attached Gleipnir to a heavy chain which they ran through a hole in a large rock. Fenris opened his mouth extraordinarily wide and attempted to bite at the gods while they were fastening the chain, so they placed a sword in his jaw, it's hilt in his lower jaw and it's point in his upper. Fenris howls terribly, and the slaver running from his mouth forms a river. He will remain chained until Ragnarok.

Freya's Necklace

Freya was the daughter of the Vanir god Njord and was the sister of Frey. She was the goddess of love and music. One night Freya crept out of her hall and quietly left Asgard, followed, unknown to her, by the giant-god Loki. She found her way to the land of the dwarves (Nithavellir) and then to the smithy of four dwarves - Alfrigg, Dvalin, Berling and Grerr. These four dwarves were said to represent the four elements – earth, air, fire and water.

The dwarves were making a golden necklace, carved with wondrous patterns. It was the most beautiful thing Freya had ever seen and she desired it more than she desired anything before or after. She offered to buy the necklace, but the dwarves would accept nothing less than a date with the goddess of love for each of them. Freya agreed to this, and after the four dates, returned to her hall under the cover of darkness with the necklace. It was called the called the Brisingamen.

Loki, having witnessed the entire transaction, made straight for Odin's hall and told the All-Father what Freya had done. Odin was furious (it seems he and Freya may have been dating) and ordered Loki to get the necklace from Freya. Loki did this by shape-shifting into a fly, entering Freya's home, and stealing the necklace from her as she lay asleep.

When Freya woke the next morning she realized the necklace had been stolen from her. She knew that only Loki was capable of such an act and that moreover, he would have only done such a thing at Odin's behest. She hurried to Odin and confronted him about the necklace, whereupon Odin told her that he had the Brisingamen and that she could only see it again if she used her magic to start a war on earth, then caused the warriors who fell dead to return to life and fight again. Freya agreed to this and her necklace was returned. It was considered the most valuable possession of all the gods. At one point, Thor even borrowed the Brisingamen to pretend to be Freya in order to regain his stolen hammer.

Recovery of Thor's Hammer

Once upon a time it happened that Thor's great hammer, Mjollnir, fell into the possession of the king of the frost giants, Thrym. Because Thor's hammer had killed so many of his bretheren, Thrym took Mjollnir and buried it eight fathoms deep under the rocks of Jotunheim, the land of the giants. Knowing the giants would attack him on sight and that he would be in peril without his hammer, Thor sent Loki to negotiate with Thrym. Loki argued and pleaded with his giant relative, but could only prevail so far as to get the giant's promise to restore the weapon if Freya, the goddess of love, would consent to be his bride.

Loki returned and reported the result of his mission to the gods. Freya was quite horrified at the idea of giving her hand to the king of the frost giants. In this emergency, Loki persuaded Thor to dress himself in Freya's clothes and accompany him back to Jotunheim. Thor wore a veil over his face to disguise himself. Freya even gave Thor her famous Brisings necklace to complete the disguise.

Back in Jotunheim, the frost giant Thrym received his veiled bride with due courtesy, but was greatly surprised at seeing her eat eight salmon and a full-grown ox for supper. His amazement continued when she washed the whole meal down with three barrels of mead. Loki, however, assured Thrym that "Freya" had not tasted anything for eight long nights, so great was her desire to see her groom.

After a while, Thrym's curiosity got the best of him and he peeped under his bride's veil, but started back in fright and demanded to know why Freya's eyeballs burned with fire. Loki repeated the same excuse, that she was filled with a burning desire to marry him and the giant seemed satisfied.

Believing that Loki had met his demands, Thrym ordered Thor's hammer to be brought in and laid on the "Freya's" lap. At once, Thor threw off his disguise, grasped his famous weapon, and proceeded to slaughter Thrym and all his followers.

Building of Asgard's Wall

The gods realized they needed to rebuild the wall that had surrounded Asgard, as it had been destroyed during the war between the Aesir and the Vanir. While the gods were talented and well skilled in building magnificent halls and buildings, they thought the task of building a fortress-like wall beyond them. One day a tall man came across Bifrost and told Heimdall that he had a plan to bring before the gods. (Only Thor was missing on a trip.) Odin gathered all the gods and goddesses to meet with the stranger and hear his plan. The stranger (a giant in disguise) said he could rebuild the wall surrounding Asgard in 18 months. For payment he would take the sun and moon and also Freya as his wife. Odin became angry and said the gods would never give up Freya, nor would they give up the sun and moon. He angrily bid the mason leave.

However, Loki begged the gods not to be so hasty and he asked the mason for some time to consider his offer. When the stranger left, all the gods and goddesses gathered around and Loki suggested they get the mason to agree to build the wall in six months. If not, he would not be paid. Loki explained there was no way the mason would be able to complete the task in the time allotted, but he would get a portion of the work done, thereby making it easier for the gods to finish the task and the gods wouldn't have to pay.

This sounded like a good idea, so Odin called the mason back into the hall and put Loki's plan before him. The mason seemed hesitant, but said he would agree to the terms if he was allowed to use his horse, Svadilfari to help him. The gods agreed and the bargain was struck.

The mason set to work on the first day of winter and had his horse draw stone for the building. The gods saw that he was making amazing progress on the construction. The mason cut huge blocks of stone and the horse hauled loads heavier than anything the gods had seen. Throughout the winter the wall began to take shape. The gods became worried, but had sworn solemn oaths to the mason. Without these precautions he would not have thought himself safe among the gods, especially if Thor should return from his journey.

Near the end of winter the building was far advanced and the bulwarks were sufficiently high and massive to render the place impregnable. In short, when it wanted but three days to summer, the only part that remained to be finished was the gateway. The gods realized the wall would soon be completed and they would have to give up Freya along with the sun and moon. The gods shouted angrily at Loki as it was his idea that led to this. Because of his bad counsel they planned to put him to a cruel death unless he fixed the problem.

Three nights before the solstice, Svadilfari was hauling the last of the stones toward the wall when another horse suddenly ran out of a forest and began to neigh. Svadilfari broke loose and ran after the horse into the forest, which obliged the mason to run after them both. The mason chased them all night but could not catch up. The next day he had not made the usual progress on the wall. When he realized he would not be able to complete his work on time, he resumed his normal gigantic stature and stormed into Asgard shouting and raving. The gods now clearly perceived that it was a mountain giant who had come amongst them so they called on Thor, who had just returned from his journey. Lifting up his hammer, he paid the workman his wages, not the sun and moon and Freya, but with the first blow he shattered the giant's skull to pieces and hurled him headlong into Niflheim.

Several months later Loki returned to Asgard leading a young colt that had eight legs. This magnificent animal could run on land or in the air. The colt was the offspring of Svadilfari (the giant's horse) and Loki, who had disguised himself to lead it away. Odin took the colt for his own and named him Sleipnir.

Idunn's Apples and the Marriage of Skadi

Once three of the gods, Odin, Loki, and Hoenir had left Asgard and traveled throughout the world without any provisions. Coming to a valley they saw a herd of oxen so they took one and set about to cooking it. When they thought it was ready they removed it from the fire, but it was not cooked. They placed it back on the fire to cook longer but when they removed it a second time it was still uncooked. They began to discuss what could cause such a thing when they heard a voice up in an oak tree above them. They looked up and saw a large eagle sitting in the tree. The eagle said, "If you agree to give me my fill of the ox, then your meat will get cooked." The gods agreed to this and the eagle sailed down to snatch up two thighs and both the shoulders of the ox.

Loki grew angry at this and he grabbed a great stick and drove it deep into the eagle's body. The eagle recoiled from the attack and flew up into the air with one end of the stick firmly in its back and Loki clinging to the other end. The eagle was flying just high enough for Loki's feet to be dragging along the stones and bushes on the ground and he (Loki) thought his arms would be pulled from their sockets. He called out to the eagle asking for mercy but the eagle replied it would only release Loki if he would swear an oath to bring Idunn and her apples out of Asgard. Loki agreed and so was released and allowed to return to his companions.

Upon his return to Asgard, Loki went to Idunn and told her that during his journeys he had found some apples that were more golden and beautiful than hers. He suggested they take some of her apples and go compare them to the ones he had found. Not suspecting treachery, Idunn agreed and they set out from Asgard. It was then that the giant Thiassi came in the form of the eagle and carried Idunn away.

The gods were dismayed at the disappearance of Idunn for, without her apples, they would grow old and grey. They held an assembly and asked who had last seen Idunn. Heimdall said he had last seen her leaving Asgard in the company of Loki. Loki, who wasn't there, was seized and brought before the assembly and made to tell what he had done. The assembly threatened him with torture and death and he grew so frightened that he said he would journey to Jotunheim to retrieve Idunn if Freya would lend him her falcon coat.

With the falcon coat he used it to transform into a falcon and he flew to Jotunheim. He arrived on a day when Thiassi had gone out rowing on the sea and Idunn was home alone. Loki changed her into the form of a nut and, holding her in his talons, flew off at top speed. When Thiassi

returned home and saw that Idunn was missing he took the shape of an eagle and flew after Loki with a tremendous rush of air in his wake. The gods, seeing the falcon flying with the nut and the eagle in pursuit, went out to the walls of Asgard carrying bundles of wood shavings. When the falcon (Loki) reached Asgard he dropped down at the wall and the gods set fire to the plane shavings. The eagle (Thiassi) was unable to check his course and he flew through the flames causing his feathers to catch fire. He fell to the ground and the gods gathered around and killed him inside the gates. So Idunn was returned to Asgard where she continues to distribute the golden apples that allow the gods to maintain their youth.

But the tale does not end there. When the frost-giantess, Skadi, daughter of Thiassi, heard of her father's death, she immediately set out for Asgard with her weapons to attack the gods. So great was her wrath that the gods tried to appease Skadi by allowing her to marry one of them. She was to choose her husband by looking only at their feet. Skadi tried to choose the feet of Balder, the most handsome of the gods. However the feet she picked belonged to, Njord, god of fishing and father of Frey and Freya. Skadi was upset, until someone played a practical joke on Loki, making Skadi laugh for the first time in her life. To make her feel better, Odin took her father's eyes and threw them in the sky to create two new stars.

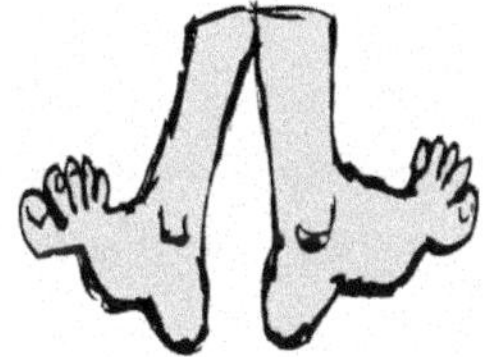

So Skadi married Njord, but the marriage did not turn out well. Njord preferred to live near the sea, while Skadi preferred to live in her mountain home. Skadi didn't like the sea, because the sound of the seagulls kept her awake, while Njord complained about the howling of the wolves in the mountains.

Frey and Gerda

One day in Asgard, Frey, god of the harvest, sat on Odin's throne. From there, he could see into the giant Gymir's home in Jotunheim, and he saw Gerda, the beautiful daughter of Gymir. Frey instantly fell in love with her and became sick because of his longing for the beautiful giantess.

Njord, Frey's father, and Skadi, his stepmother, became concerned when they noticed Frey's longing and depression. Skadi asked Frey's shield-bearer, Skirnir, to try and help their son.

At first, Frey refused to talk about what was bothering him, even to Skirnir, but finally, after Skirnir assured Frey that he would do anything to help him Frey told the tale. "I have seen and fallen in love with Gerda in the land of Jotunheim, but I do not know how to approach her with a proposal of marriage."

Skirnir told Frey that he would woo Gerda for him, if the god would loan him his horse for the journey and give him his magic sword as the price for his services. Frey possessed this wonderful weapon which dwarves had made, a sword that would move on its own volition during battle if its master's mind was wise enough.

So smitten was Frey that he agreed to Skirnir's terms. Skirnir rode to Gymir's domain, seeking an audience with Gerda. Though delighted with a visitor, her welcome became cold when Gerda learned that Skirnir's mission was to woo her for Frey. Though Frey was among the most handsome gods, Gerda did not care for him.

At first, Skirnir offered her gifts, so that she would consider Frey's suit favorably. Skirnir promised eleven golden apples (probably Idunn's apple of youth), but Gerda flatly refused. Then Skirnir offered her a magic gold ring that will make eight identical copies of itself every nine nights. This was obviously Draupnir; the ring that belonged to Odin. Again, Gerda refused the gift; she had enough gold in her father's home.

When none of these gifts seemed suitable for Gerda, Skirnir decided to try threats, hoping to bully her in accepting Frey's suit. Skirnir told her that he would use Frey's sword to chop off her head if she refused to marry. But, since Gerda was a giantess and surrounded by her father's people, this threat fell on deaf ears.

Finally, Skirnir threatened to put a curse on Gerda. He said he would transform her into a three-headed giantess, her face and body made old and hideously ugly. It was only the threat of this curse that finally moved Gerda to agree to marry Frey. She promised to meet him in nine nights in a valley.

Skirnir returned with the news to Frey. Frey was upset and impatient that he had to wait for nine more nights before he could meet Gerda. He said, "Long is one night, Long are two nights, How shall I hold out three? Shorter hath seemed a month to me...." Eventually, however, the wait was over and Gerda met and married Frey as she had promised.

So Frey obtained Gerda, the most beautiful of all giantesses, for his wife, but at the cost of his enchanted sword. For love, Frey had deprived himself of his only chance to defeat the fire-giant Surt, at the battle of Ragnarok.

Thor's Journey to Jotunheim

One night Thor and Loki were on a journey in Thor's chariot. They came to a farmer's home where they received lodging for the night. Thor killed and skinned his own goats and cooked them. He told the farmer and his household to toss the bones whole upon the skins on the ground when they were done eating. But Thialfi, the farmer's son, took a thigh bone and split it open to get at the marrow. In the morning, when Thor took blessed the goat skins with Mjollnir, the goats returned to life, but one was lame. Thor was enraged and the farmer and his family grew afraid. When Thor saw their terror he calmed down and accepted their son as settlement. So Thor, Loki, and Thialfi continued on the journey.

As darkness came they found shelter in a strange building, but were awakened at midnight by a great earthquake. When the dawn arrived Thor went out and discovered the source of the shaking was a snoring giant asleep nearby. The giant awoke and stood and it is said that for once Thor was afraid to strike with Mjollnir. Instead, he asked the giant his name. The giant said he was called Skrymir and asked if Thor was trying to steal his glove. Then Skrymir reached over and picked up the strange building Thor and his companions had spent the night in, which was, indeed, the giant's glove. Skrymir asked if Thor and his companions wished to travel with him and Thor agreed. Later that evening Skrymir found lodging for them all beneath a giant oak tree.

While Skrymir went to sleep, Thor tried to untie Skrymir's sack to cook some food. But no matter how hard he labored, he couldn't loosen a single knot or move a single strap. Growing angry, Thor took Mjollnir and struck Skrymir in the head. The giant awoke and asked if a leaf had fallen on him.

At midnight Thor was awakened by Skrymir's snoring. He got up and swung his hammer at the center of Skrymir's forehead. When Skrymir awoke he only asked if an acorn had fallen on his head. Just before dawn the giant was still deep asleep so Thor rose up, ran at Skrymir, and swung Mjollnir with all his might. This time Skrymir woke and stroked his cheek asking if there were any birds in the tree above him dropping twigs. At sunrise, Skrymir said goodbye and left for the mountains to the north.

Thor and his companions set off to the east and by midday saw a castle standing in an open field. They had to bend their heads far back to see the top. Thor tried open the gate, but when he could not, they had to squeeze between the bars. Once inside they saw a great number of giants seated on two benches. The giant king, Utgartha, said, "Am I wrong in thinking that this little fellow is Thor? You must be bigger than you look to me." He asked what feats they would perform to be allowed to stay.

Loki said that he could eat faster than anyone. Utgartha smiled and called forth Logi. A trencher piled with meat was set between them. Loki and Logi sat at opposite ends and ate as quickly as they could. They met in the middle and while Loki had eaten all the meat on his half, Logi had devoured the meat, bones and the trencher itself.

Next, Thialfi said he would run a race with anyone. Utgartha called forth a boy named Hugi and bade him run three races with Thialfi. They started the first race and Hugi was soon so far ahead that he had to turn and run backwards to cross the finish line. Try as he might, Thialfi lost every one of three races.

Thor then said he would engage in a drinking contest with anyone. Utgartha called for the drinking horn. Thor took the it and began to drink with great gulps. When he ran out of breath he looked and saw that there was very little difference in the level. Determined to drink a bigger draught, he struggled with the horn as long as his breath would hold out. When he lowered the horn and looked into it, the level in the horn had gone down less than the previous time. Utgartha said Thor had given a poor accounting of himself. At this, Thor grew angry and handed the horn back saying he would drink no more.

Utgartha then said it was clear that Thor was not as great as they had heard, but maybe he would try a game the young giants played of trying to lift his cat off the ground. A big grey cat ran into the hall and Thor took hold with one hand under its belly and lifted it up. But the cat arched its back as Thor pulled and in the end the cat had lifted only one paw from the floor. Utgartha said the contest had gone as he expected since the cat was rather big and Thor was short. Thor responded by saying, "Small as you say I am, just let someone come out and fight me! Now I am angry!"

Utgartha looked about the hall and seeing no one small enough to fight with Thor, called for his old nurse, Elli. They began to wrestle, but the harder Thor strained against her, the firmer she stood. Then the old woman started trying some tricks and Thor began to lose his footingand soon fell to one knee. Utgartha then stopped the contest, declaring Elli the winner. It was now late and Utgartha showed Thor and his companions to where they could spend the night.

When dawn came they got up and dressed, preparing to set off when Utgartha came to walk them out of the castle. He asked how Thor felt about his journey and Thor replied, "I know you will say I am a person of little account and it is that which upsets me." Then Utgartha said, "Now that we are outside the castle I can tell you the truth. You would never have been allowed in if I had known what strength you possessed." He told Thor how he had deceived him seven times. First, he had been the giant who met them in the forest. The sack had been fastened with a trick wire. Each time Thor struck him with Mjollnir, he had moved an invisible mountain in its path.

The contests in the castle, Utgartha said, were also rigged. Loki's opponent was really wildfire

which eats up everything. Thialfi had raced against the speed of thought. The drinking horn had been connected to the sea which as now considerably lower (we now call this the tides). When Thor attempted to lift the cat from the floor, it was no cat, but was Jormmugand, the serpent that encircles the world. When Thor was wrestling with Elli, he was actually wrestling against old age and not even a god can conquer that. Utgartha then said that it would be better that Thor never return to Utgard for next time he would defend his castle with similar tricks and Thor could never win.

Upon hearing all this Thor grasped his hammer to strike but Utgartha was gone. He turned for the castle, intending to destroy it, but the castle was gone as well. He then headed back to Asgard, determined to challenge Jormmugand again and he did as is told in the story Thor Goes Fishing.

Thor Goes Fishing

One day the gods decided to hold a feast and they decided that Aegir, god of the sea, would host it for them. But the gods' tone annoyed Aegir who said that he did not have a cauldron big enough to brew enough ale to be able to invite everyone. Tyr, the one-handed god of battle, suggested that they go get a magic cauldron, which would allow Aegir to brew unlimited ale.

Aegir liked the idea so much that he sent Thor and Tyr to fetch the cauldron. The problem was that the giant Hymir possessed it. Thor and Tyr traveled to Hymir's hall, where the first person they encountered Hymir's 900-headed mother.

At dinner, Thor astonished the company by devouring two entire oxen. The next morning, Hymir said that if they were to eat again together, they would need to get more food. Thor suggested going fishing and asked for bait from Hymir. The giant told him to find his own and pointed to his field. So Thor tore off the head of Hymir's finest ox to use as bait.

The giant and the god rowed out to sea in Hymir's small boat. Thor kept urging Hymir to row further and further from shore. Finally, Hymir refused to row one stroke more. While Hymir caught and landed two whales, Thor caught Jormmugand, the serpent that encircles the world. A titanic struggle between the thunder god and the Midgard Serpent erupted, causing the boat to rock dangerously. Hymir was horrified when Thor brought the serpent's head out of the water. As the god and serpent faced one another, Thor tried to smash his hammer on monster's head.

Hymir, who was frightened almost to death by the size of the monster, used his knife to cut off Thor's line. Thor threw Mjollnir at Jormmugand's head, but failed to kill the serpent. Thor was angry with the giant for allowing Jormmugand to escape and he struck Hymir with his fist, knocking him out of the boat and into the water.

Eventully, the two returned to shore. Hymir asked Thor if he wanted carry the two whales to the hall or drag the boat up past the high tide line. In reply, Thor dragged the boat, the two whales, and Hymir himself back to the hall.

Hymir could see that he had come off second best and so challenged Thor to smash a glass goblet as a test of strength. Thor threw the goblet at a stone pillar, but it was the pillar that broke into bits. Hymir's wife whispered to Thor that he should throw the goblet at Hymir's head, which was harder than any rock. Thor did so, smashing the goblet. Realizing he had lost to the thunder god, Hymir gave his prized cauldron to Thor. Tyr could not even lift the cauldron off the ground, but Thor easily carried the cauldron on top of his head.

Hymir and his companions disliked losing to Thor, so they pursued the two gods into the forest. Thor realizing the danger, decided to confront them at once. Being Thor, he killed Hymir and all the giants who had followed him.

Thor and Tyr brought the magic cauldron back to Aegir's hall beneath the sea. Aegir was so happy to have it that he forgot his anger with the gods and still brews ale for them even today.

Ragnarok

Ragnarok is the end. The doom of gods and elves, of men and giants alike. It is the final battle of good verses evil. The Aesir (the gods of Asgard, lead by Odin) would fight for good; Loki and the giants would fight for the side of evil. Strangely enough, most of the outcomes are already

known. Prophecies have been given and all the gods and goddesses know who will survive and who will be killed by whom.

Prophecies foretell the beginning of Ragnarok, as well as the outcome. Before the Great War begins three winters will pass with no summers between. In this winter of winters conflict and feuding will run rampant -- even between blood-kin. Then the world will be plunged into darkness as the mighty wolf, Skoll, finally catches up and devours the sun. His twin, Hati, soon swallows the moon, as well. Then the roosters will begin to crow: one will crow to the giants, one to the gods, and one to wake the dead of Niflheim.

Earthquakes will rend the ground and shake the world with such ferocity that the monstrous wolf Fenris will be freed of his enchanted chain. Every bond will

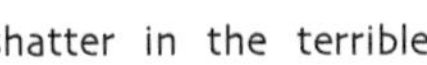

shatter in the terrible quakes. The seas will erupt as the Midgard Serpent, Jormmugand, strains and writhes -- trying to make his way to the shore. Heimdall will sound his horn, Gjallahorn.

That keening will draw all the competitors to the last battle: the sons of Odin, the heroes, the gods, giants, dwarves, and elves. They will converge in the plain of Vigrid ("the Battle Shaker") in a hopeless war.

Frey, without his magical sword and totally unarmed, would be the first god to be killed in battle with Surt (the great fire giant). Odin will be swallowed by Fenris. Odin's son, Vidar, will then rip Fenris' jaws apart with his bare hands. Thor and Jormmugand (the Midgard Serpent) will fight one final time. Thor will kill Jormmugand with his hammer, but

later die from the poison bites he receives. Tyr and Garm (a great hound) will kill each other, as will Loki and Heimdall.

Then Surt, who carries a magic sword that burns as bright as noon-day sun, will fling fire across all the Nine Worlds and burn everyone and everything left standing , friend and foe alike.

Two humans, Lif and Lifthrasir, hide in the sacred tree called Yggdrasil during the battle and don't return until after it is over. When they emerge, they repopulate the Earth. Other survivors of Ragnarok include a few gods, particularly Odin's sons Vidar and Vali and Thor's sons Modi and Magni. Another of Odin's sons, Balder, will be revived from the dead after the battle. So life will go on, but only in a new and different age.

www.ingramcontent.com/pod-product-compliance
Ingram Content Group UK Ltd.
Pitfield, Milton Keynes, MK11 3LW, UK
UKHW020235250726
13967UKWH00001B/371

9 781257 837298